How to Play
HARMONICA

How to Play
HARMONICA

A Complete Guide for Beginners

BLAKE BROCKSMITH, GARY DORFMAN, and DOUGLAS LICHTERMAN

ADAMS MEDIA

NEW YORK   LONDON   TORONTO   SYDNEY   NEW DELHI

Adams Media
An Imprint of Simon & Schuster, Inc.
57 Littlefield Street
Avon, Massachusetts 02322

First Adams Media trade paperback edition APRIL 2018

ADAMS MEDIA and colophon are trademarks of Simon and Schuster.

For information about special discounts for bulk purchases, please contact Simon & Schuster Special Sales at 1-866-506-1949 or business@simonandschuster.com.

The Simon & Schuster Speakers Bureau can bring authors to your live event. For more information or to book an event contact the Simon & Schuster Speakers Bureau at 1-866-248-3049 or visit our website at www.simonspeakers.com.

Interior design by Colleen Cunningham
Interior illustrations by Mark DiVico

Manufactured in the United States of America

10 9 8 7 6 5 4 3 2 1

Library of Congress Cataloging-in-Publication Data
Brocksmith, Blake, author. | Dorfman, Gary, author. | Lichterman, Douglas, author.
How to play harmonica / Blake Brocksmith, Gary Dorfman, and Douglas Lichterman.
Avon, Massachusetts: Adams Media, 2018.
Series: How to play.
Includes bibliographical references and index.
LCCN 2017055484 | ISBN 9781507206645 (pb) | ISBN 9781507206652 (ebook)
LCSH: Harmonica--Instruction and study.
LCC MT682 .B76 2018 | DDC 788.8/2193--dc23
LC record available at https://lccn.loc.gov/2017055484

ISBN 978-1-5072-0664-5
ISBN 978-1-5072-0665-2 (ebook)

Contains material adapted from the following title published by Adams Media, an Imprint of Simon & Schuster, Inc.: *The Everything® Harmonica Book with CD* by Douglas Lichterman, Blake Brocksmith, and Gary Dorfman, copyright © 2008, ISBN 978-1-59869-482-6.

CONTENTS

INTRODUCTION

Have you heard an amazing harmonica riff on one of your favorite songs? Want to figure out how to play one yourself? You've come to the right place. You don't have to know anything about the harmonica to get started with this book, but even if you have been playing for a little while you'll find that this book contains plenty of useful information to improve your understanding, technique, and musicianship.

What's not to love about the harmonica? It's inexpensive, portable, and full of rich sound. The instrument was an instant hit when first introduced in the United States around the mid-1800s. Back then, it was a favorite of cowboys, soldiers, hobos, and just about anybody with a pocket. Nowadays, the harmonica is still a vital sound in many albums, such as *Flight of the Cosmic Hippo* by Béla Fleck and the Flecktones and *Four* by Blues Traveler. Modern harmonica players, such as Frédéric Yonnet (a French harmonica player who has recorded with Erykah Badu, Ed Sheeran, and John Legend, among others), continue to amass large fan bases.

The harmonica is well known in blues and folk music, but it also appears in jazz, rock, country, and classical, and its sphere of musical genres is still growing. You can even hear sampled harmonica on hip-hop albums, such as Bad News Brown's *Born 2 Sin*, as well as on techno albums. Sounds you'd never believe could be produced by a harmonica appear in some modern rock songs. Whatever style of music you want to play, there's a way to fit harmonica into it.

One reason the harmonica is especially fun is that anyone can get nice sound out of a harmonica on the first attempt. Sure, there's a lot to learn beyond that, but this book will walk you through everything you need to know.

Now it's your turn to enter the intense, vibrant, and electrifying world of harmonica music with *How to Play Harmonica* as your guide.

HOW TO USE THIS BOOK

To get the most out of this book you should know about some of the notation and terms used throughout. You may have seen some of it before, and some of it may be new to you.

Standard Notation and Harmonica Tablature

In musical notation there is one line of standard notation written on the staff and one line of harmonica tablature below it. Note that the harmonica tab by nature does not indicate rhythmic notation, so you'll have to use the standard notation to get that information. Harmonica tab only indicates which hole on the harmonica to play, whether it's a blow note or a draw note, and what kind of bend, if any, to use (more on bends in Chapter 2).

Harmonica Diagrams

Harmonica diagrams are used to illustrate the harmonica itself. They show a front view of the harmonica, with the ten holes indicated and numbered. Hole 1, which appears on the left side of the diagram, is the lowest-pitch note, and hole 10, which appears on the right side, is the highest-pitch note.

HARMONICA HERO: LITTLE WALTER

Marion Walter Jacobs (1930–1968), known as Little Walter, is widely regarded as the most influential harmonica player of the 1940s and 1950s. He transformed the sound of the harmonica through both his electrifying technique and his innovation of using an amplifier and a Green Bullet microphone (now the most popular harmonica mic in the world largely because of him) to get a purposely distorted sound out of the harmonica. Little Walter's sound was smooth and sustained and sounded as much like a saxophone as a harp. He also added the critical innovation of cupping his hands around the back of the harmonica, which added further distortion to his unique sound. In 1964 he toured Europe with the Rolling Stones. He died in Chicago in 1968 after being in a street fight.

Chapter 1

ONE NOTE AT A TIME

First, this chapter examines the different types of harmonicas available to help you become familiar with the instrument and choose the one that's best for you. Next, it covers the fundamentals of reading music to get you started or as a refresher if you're not new to music. Finally, it focuses on some of the specific techniques you'll need to learn to take command of your new instrument. These include controlling your breath, shaping your mouth, and using your tongue in order to produce the notes and sounds you want, as well as the proper way to hold the instrument. The goal is to get clean single notes out of your harmonica.

Types of Harmonicas

Let's talk briefly about the different types of harmonicas. There are two basic kinds: diatonic and chromatic. They differ in how the reeds are tuned when the "harp" is made. (There are many further variations within these two categories, but we'll stick with the basics here.)

HARP TIP

A reed in a harmonica is a piece of thin metal that vibrates to produce sounds when air is blown on it. Reeds are also found in mouthpieces of clarinets and oboes, and in accordions.

Chromatic

The chromatic harmonica is a more advanced style of harmonica. It has a button on the side that allows the musician to control the number of notes available to play. When you press the button, you can play all the major notes in a scale, plus the half steps (or notes in between). When the button isn't pressed, you can only play the major notes. The chromatic harmonica is used most often in jazz and classical music.

Diatonic

The diatonic harmonica is a simpler harmonica because it doesn't have a complete selection of notes like the chromatic harmonica (although many of the notes that are not naturally found on it can be acquired by "bending" certain notes like blues players do—you'll learn about bending in Chapter 2). Most professional harmonica players are diatonic players. It is typically used in blues, rock, country, and folk, but it can be found in all styles of music. The diatonic harmonica is sometimes called a blues harp, short harp, or standard ten-hole. This book uses a C diatonic harmonica for teaching purposes.

Most people learn on (and often stay with) diatonic harps because they are designed to never have a wrong note. This is accomplished by leaving out some of the tones from the chromatic scale and using only the diatonic scale. Diatonic takes only the notes that create chords and leaves out the others. (The difference between the diatonic and chromatic scales is that diatonic contains only five of the tones of a given scale while chromatic contains all eight.) What is important to remember is that some notes do not exist naturally on the diatonic scale, which is the scale this book focuses on.

HARP TIP

In music theory, two notes played at the same time make an *interval*, and three or more notes played at the same time make a *chord*. Major and minor chords are made up of intervals called *thirds*, which are formed when you play two notes of a scale that are separated by one note. For example, a C major scale is made up of the notes C, D, E, F, G, A, B, C. If you play the notes C and E together, omitting the D in between, you have a third. Playing D and F together or E and G together also make thirds, and so on.

Reading Music

How will you know exactly what notes to play? Through a type of musical notation called *tablature*. Tablature is a form of notation specific to the harmonica that tells you exactly what to do and when. There are only two ways to draw sound from a harmonica: by blowing and by drawing. When you blow out through the reeds it makes a sound, and when you draw (or suck) in air it creates another sound. Blowing is represented in tablature by an up arrow, and drawing is represented by a down arrow, as shown in the following image.

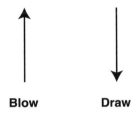

Blow   **Draw**

Air Direction

FIGURE 1-1. BLOW AND DRAW ARROW SYMBOLS

HARP TIP

A diatonic scale is one with eight notes from octave to octave, which contains only the notes in the scale of the key being played. A chromatic scale is one with thirteen notes from octave to octave, which includes every possible note in the scale that exists between the two octaves.

Next there are single notes, shown on the harmonica by the numbers over the holes. So if the song or exercise wants you to play the 2 hole by drawing air, you will see 2↓. The number corresponds to the number that usually appears on the upper plate of the harmonica and the arrow indicates what to do with your breath.

BLOW NOTES

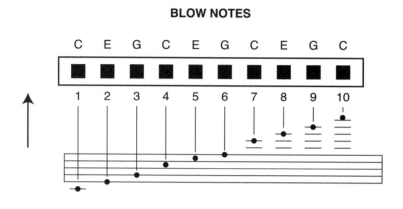

DRAW NOTES

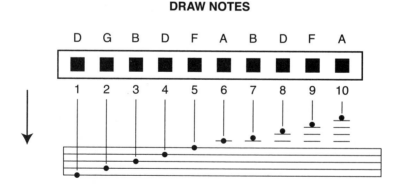

FIGURE 1-2. HOLES 1–10, WITH BLOW AND DRAW NOTES

There are a number of different ways to draw and blow through the harp, and you will learn some of those techniques in Chapter 2.

Get Comfortable with the Instrument

The first thing you'll notice when picking up a harmonica is how easy it is to play chords that sound good right off the bat. This is one big reason why the harmonica has become such a popular instrument in folk music as well as in rock and jazz, and why hundreds of millions of them have been manufactured over the years.

Spending some time just breathing through your harmonica is a good way to get a sense of how the instrument feels and the degree to which you feel comfortable with it. In fact, it can be very relaxing just to breathe through the low end (holes 1, 2, and 3) of the instrument and listen to the hypnotic alternating chords your breath produces as it blows and draws over the reeds. This is also a good focusing exercise to shift your mind from the other concerns of your day to preparing to play the harmonica.

HARMONICA HERO: JOHN POPPER

John Popper (b. 1967) is one of the leading harmonica virtuosos in the contemporary music scene. As the singer, harmonica player, songwriter, and founding member of Blues Traveler, Popper has been thrilling audiences for years with his dazzling and hyperactive harp style, born from listening to great jazz improvisers. His musicianship has pushed the harmonica to the forefront of soloing instruments in the modern rock setting. Here's a fun story about him: As a high school student, John Popper ran in a student election. When his turn came to make a speech he pulled out a harmonica and started to wail. The crowd responded with wild applause and dancing. But instead of winning the election, Popper got suspended from school. Popper has also been a leading proponent of the use of effects to create his harmonica sound, using devices including wah-wahs, fuzz tones, synthesizers, digital delays, and octave generators to stretch the limits of what is possible on the instrument.

If you then play around a little by just blowing and drawing chords up and down the instrument you'll begin to understand what your harmonica is capable of doing, and how your breath affects the low, middle, and high reeds differently. As you get up to the higher reeds and the space the air is coming through becomes smaller, the amount of air you can blow or draw through the reed is reduced, and thus you'll find it takes less air to move the reed and get the note. Consequently you'll be inhaling or exhaling less volume of air when playing at the higher end of the harp and using more volume of air when playing at the lower end.

HARMONICA HERO: BIG WALTER HORTON

Big Walter "Shakey" Horton (1921–1981) was a harmonica luminary said to be one of the best blues harp players of all time. Besides developing a unique hornlike tone on the instrument and a completely distinctive virtuoso style, Horton was one of the earliest proponents of the amplified harmonica sound that defined Chicago-style blues, claiming to have begun using an amplifier around 1940. He was also a teacher and mentor to many players, including harmonica icons Little Walter and Sonny Boy Williamson II, and later to top players Peter "Madcat" Ruth and Carey Bell. Horton's most famous recording was an instrumental track recorded with guitarist Jimmy DeBerry called "Easy," which became his biggest hit and is considered to be one of the best harmonica recordings of all time.

Mastering Breath Control

You'll notice as you play that you can only get a pleasant sound out of the reed when you're using just the right amount of breath. Use too much and it sounds forced, and the reed also may stick at times. Use too little and it sounds weak and breathy—*not* the sound you're going for. Throughout this book you will practice exercises and riffs that are going to teach you about breath control.

HARP TIP

Spending extended periods practicing breath control can be difficult if you have trouble breathing from asthma or other respiratory problems, or even if you have no respiratory problems at all. Be careful not to overdo it.

Diaphragmatic Breathing

Singers use a technique called diaphragmatic breathing that can also be useful for harmonica players. The diaphragm is a band of muscle just below your lungs. Try breathing in deeply with your hand on your stomach and see if you can make your hand move outward with your stomach using only your breath. Feel it as you do, then expel the air slowly and deliberately until you feel you cannot exhale anymore. Do this exercise three times in a row. When you're doing it correctly you will feel noticeably full of air, and if you practice this regularly you'll have more breath to control as well as better ability to control it. Many experienced harmonica players do this before they begin to practice to wake up their lungs.

HARP TIP

You might find as you're playing that you either run completely out of air or your lungs become full from playing draw notes. To avoid this, take or expel small breaths right on the beat. (A beat is a rhythmic unit in music.) Any of the beats of the measure will do for this, although you might find that the 1 and 4 beats are best because they're naturally at the end of many phrases. The important thing is to do this between the phrases (i.e., a group of notes that expresses a musical thought or idea) that you're playing, as opposed to interrupting a phrase to take or expel a breath.

Focus on Breathing Through Your Mouth

Harmonica playing is an exercise in breath control. Most people breathe through their nose and mouth, or just through their nose. But if you breathe through your nose while you play the harmonica, you will not be putting all of your breath into the art of playing. Learning how *not* to breathe through your nose while playing requires that you think about it while you play, at least until it becomes second nature. This is true for diaphragmatic breathing as well.

HARP TIP

When playing draw notes on the low end of the harmonica, you might find the sound you're producing to be weak, muffled, or lower than the correct pitch. This is the result of choking the reeds by forcing too much air through them. To avoid this, reduce the amount of air you're using on the problem notes, and try adjusting your mouth and throat positions.

How to Hold Your Harmonica

Finding the most comfortable position to hold your harmonica is essential to developing your own style of play. As you consider where to put your hands, it's good to know what's inside the instrument:

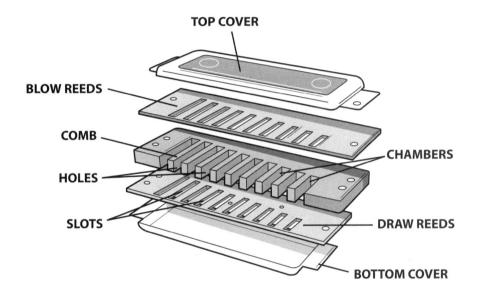

FIGURE 1-3. PARTS OF A HARMONICA

Here are some basic rules that apply when you focus on hand placement:

- Don't block the comb with your fingers—you don't want your hands to impede airflow through the instrument.
- Begin by holding it on one or both sides with your thumb and forefinger. This is helpful at first because you want to see which holes you are playing when practicing techniques to get single notes.
- The standard way to hold the harmonica is to place the left side of the harp into the crook between your thumb and forefinger in a comfortable but

firm way, allowing your thumb to hold up the base of the harp and your finger to run along the top. You want to still be able to see the hole numbers on the top plate going from 1 to 10 from left to right (i.e., assuming you are using a standard ten-hole diatonic harmonica).

• Be sure to leave space for your lips on the two outer plates.

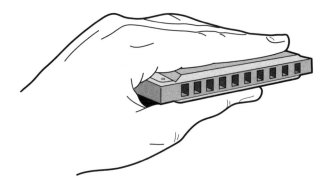

FIGURE 1-4. HOLDING THE HARMONICA

Notice that your three remaining fingers are sort of just hanging out and don't seem to be doing anything except maybe getting in the way. Hold your fingers together and make sort of a flat surface jutting out from the top of the harmonica. Then you can take your other hand and create a cavity in your two hands through which air can flow but which will mute the sound as it comes through the harp.

HARP TIP

The smallest harmonica manufactured is the Hohner Little Lady, which is less than 2 inches long and has four holes with eight reeds. The largest is the Hohner 48 Chord, which measures a whopping 23 inches long and has 192 holes with 384 reeds.

HARMONICA HERO: GARY PRIMICH

Gary Primich (1958–2007) was known for his dedication to the pure, old-school approach to playing blues harmonica, carrying on the rich tradition of Little Walter, Big Walter Horton, Sonny Boy Williamson I, and Sonny Boy Williamson II, while adding his own musical sensibility that made the classic approach sound fresh and modern. In 1984 Primich had become disillusioned with developments in the Chicago blues scene that moved away from the traditional sound he loved in favor of newer trends in rock and funk music. Feeling that his opportunities in Chicago were limited, Primich moved to Austin, Texas. There he formed the group the Mannish Boys with drummer Jimmy Carl Black. After two albums with that group he moved on to a solo career. Primich died in Austin in 2007, apparently from a drug overdose.

With a little practice, you can then open and close that gap while you play, creating vibrato similar to what a trumpet player does with a mute getting that "wa-wa" sound. This cavity you have created between your hands is where you will want to put a microphone. (Microphone techniques are discussed in Chapter 8.)

Techniques for Playing Single Notes

There are two commonly used techniques for playing single notes on a harmonica: lip pursing and tongue blocking. The first calls for you to use the muscles on the sides of your mouth to direct air through specific holes on the harp. The second is using your tongue to block some of the holes that your mouth encompasses to narrow your breath to a single note. Tongue blocking can also be used to create octaves where the middle notes of a chord are blocked and you play the lower and higher notes simultaneously. It's a good idea to learn both methods so that you have the broadest range of available sounds in your skill set.

Pursed-Lip Method

Embouchure is a musical term for how your mouth is used to work an instrument. It also refers to the mouthpiece of an instrument. All wind instruments, which are played by a person forcing air through them with his or her mouth, have an embouchure. Saxophones, flutes, trumpets, and harmonicas are all examples of instruments with embouchures.

In the case of the harmonica, you create the single-note embouchure by pursing the sides of your mouth, leaving the upper and lower lips loose as if you were going to kiss someone. You then place your mouth against the harmonica, allowing your upper lip to seal to the top of the harmonica and your lower lip to seal to the bottom. At this point you should be able to tighten the sides of your mouth to direct the air through a single hole. It may take a considerable amount of practice before you're able to get a clean single note using this method, but it is worth it.

HARMONICA HERO: CHARLIE MCCOY

Charlie McCoy (b. 1941) is best known for his relentless work as a studio musician based out of Nashville. During his career, he has recorded on thousands of sessions with a dazzling array of music luminaries. Although he is best known as a harmonica player who paved the way for harmonica in modern country music, he also plays many other instruments, including guitar, bass, drums, and trumpet. In 1959 McCoy launched his musical career, both recording with Roy Orbison and playing live with Stonewall Jackson's band. By the mid-1960s he was a sought-after studio musician, recording with the likes of Elvis Presley and backing Bob Dylan on four of his best-known albums. Other top musicians on the long list that McCoy recorded with include Frank Sinatra, Simon and Garfunkel, Johnny Cash, and Chet Atkins. McCoy is still an active performer and recording artist.

It is important to keep the upper and lower parts of your lips loose and not press too hard against the upper and lower plates on the harp—only press hard enough to create a seal against air escaping. The sides of the mouth are tensed to allow for directing air. Keeping your lips moist is also essential for creating a good seal to the harp and for allowing movement along its surface. You will know when the seal is correct because you will hear a clear, confident sound. It will feel controlled and will not have any associated loss of breath because of air escaping.

You might get the image of a goldfish when you look at yourself in the mirror doing this without the harp. Your tongue is used to help direct the air as well.

The back part of your tongue is pulled back as if to touch the roof of your mouth, but not quite touching it. The tongue comes down in an S shape that creates a directed flow of air, which combined with your pursed lips sends the flow of air directly through the hole. Moving your tongue back and forth will help in other ways, too, which are described in Chapter 2. Practice this until you can get clean single notes all the way up and down the harmonica, drawing and blowing.

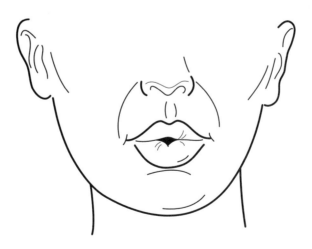

FIGURE 1-5. MOUTH IN PURSED POSITION

Tongue-Blocking Method

Tongue blocking is achieved by placing your mouth so that it covers four holes. Then, using your tongue, you block the three holes to the right or left, only allowing air to reach the fourth hole on either side of your mouth. This should produce a clean sound blowing or drawing. Practice this until you can do it on either side of your mouth, depending on which note you are trying to get. You can also try using your tongue to block only the two holes in the middle, which should produce an octave. This creates a full sound that can be very useful by playing the same note both higher and lower simultaneously.

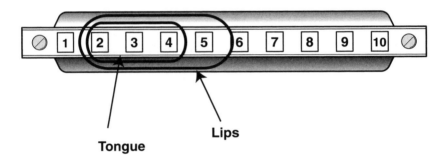

FIGURE 1-6. TONGUE-BLOCKING POSITION OF LIPS AND TONGUE

Exercises for Playing Single Notes

Here are some exercises for playing single notes on the harmonica. Achieving clean single notes on the harmonica is one of the most important parts of being able to play well.

Single Note Using Tongue Blocking

The first method that most people learn is how to play a single note by tongue blocking.

TAB: 4↓

FIGURE 1-7. SINGLE NOTE WITH TONGUE BLOCKING

Here's a simple exercise you can try to get clean notes using this method. Play each hole on your harmonica, blowing and then drawing individually. Try getting each note to sound as clean as possible before moving to the next note. Don't be discouraged if you have trouble getting clean single notes at first. With practice you'll be able to get nice, clean single notes out of every reed in your harmonica.

Single Note Using Pursed Lips

Next, try using the lip method to create a clean single note.

TAB: 1↑ 1↓ 2↑ 2↓   3↑ 3↓ 4↑ 4↓   5↑ 5↓ 6↑ 6↓   7↑ 7↓ 8↑ 8↓   9↑ 9↓ 10↑10↓

FIGURE 1-8. PURSED-LIP EXERCISE TO GET CLEAN SINGLE NOTES

29

Practicing

The ability to get a clean, strong single note on every reed of your harp is truly essential to playing well. Take a few minutes every day to practice with both the tongue method and the lip method. As you get more adept, you will also note that harmonicas of other keys have different breath thresholds. For now, just concentrate on using your harp, preferably one tuned to the key of C. (If you are not sure what key your harp is, just look at the top plate where the hole numbers are and at the right-hand corner, the key should be stamped in the metal.)

HARP TIP

President Abraham Lincoln reportedly played the harmonica and carried one around in his pocket. He even took the time while he was president to write a letter to the head of the Hohner company (a German manufacturer of musical instruments founded in 1857) expressing the joy he got from playing his Hohner harmonica.

It is a lot to take in that something so seemingly simple can be so complicated, but like every other instrument it takes time to develop skill. Strong single-note play is the basis for all the techniques that come after, so keep trying and it will come.

Chapter 2

BENDING NOTES

Now that you've learned to play single notes on the harmonica cleanly, here's something a little more advanced—bends. Bending notes is one of the most important techniques in harmonica playing. Not only is it a great tool for expressing emotion in your music, but it also adds several notes to the scale that the harmonica is capable of playing. Bending takes time to master, but once you learn the skill, it will add tremendously to your range as a player.

Bend Notations

Bending a note means changing the pitch of the note—shifting the pitch either higher or lower than the original note being played. There are six types of bends that are included in the tablature in this book: a half-step down bend, a whole-step down bend, a half-step up prebend, a dip bend down, a bump bend up, and a double bend down. These bends are indicated in the tablature with curved arrows as shown in the following figure.

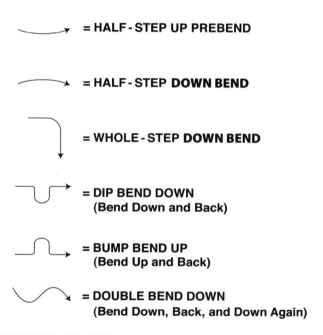

FIGURE 2-1. BEND NOTATIONS

Bent and Blue Notes on Your Harmonica

As explained in Chapter 1, there are a lot of notes in the chromatic scale that are not part of the structure of the diatonic harmonica and cannot be played as normal blow or draw notes. However, it is possible to get some of these notes by using the technique called bending. Bent notes on the harmonica are achieved by directing the force of the air through the hole in such a way that it actually creates vibration in both the draw and the blow reed at the same time. By using this method, you can create tones that occur in between the normal tones of the harmonica. These bent notes (or blue notes) are essential to playing "cross harp," or blues harmonica. Here is an example:

FIGURE 2-2. BLUES HARP EXAMPLE

HARMONICA HEROINE: CHRISSIE HYNDE

As the singer, guitarist, harmonica player, and songwriter of the Pretenders, one of rock's most beloved bands, Chrissie Hynde (b. 1951) is well known and beloved in modern music today. Hynde's scorching harmonica solos have graced many of the group's songs, the best known of which is her solo on their hit single "Middle of the Road." In addition to her considerable work on the harmonica with the Pretenders, Hynde also played harmonica with Bob Dylan and Eric Clapton at Wembley Stadium in London, England, in 1984 in a famous performance of Dylan's song "Leopard-Skin Pill-Box Hat." She also appears playing harmonica on Phil Manzanera's 2004 6PM album.

HARP TIP

The earliest blues recordings were made using wax cylinders. Thomas Edison himself, who was responsible for inventing early recording equipment, was also responsible for making many of these recordings in the early 1920s, documenting artists including the Original Memphis Five, the Georgia Melodians, Elsie Clark, and Clarence Williams with Eva Taylor.

Notes are generally bent either a half step or a whole step up or down from the original note. Bending can be done with both the draw notes and the blow notes on a harmonica and will achieve notes in between the notes built into the harp.

Many of these "in-between" notes are referred to as blue notes, which are the notes that give the blues its classic sound. Blue notes are changes made to the major scale, specifically a flatted third and a flatted seventh note, which create harmonic tension between sounds usually identified with a major scale and a minor scale. The resulting sound is the classic blues sound. A flatted fifth is also frequently used as an additional blue note. A flatted note means a note that's lowered one half step, and the terms third, fifth, and seventh refer to the position of the notes in the scale. In the case of the C major scale, which the C diatonic harmonica is based on, the notes of the scale are C, D, E, F, G, A, B, C. As you can see, the third note of the scale is the E, the fifth note is the G, and the seventh note is the B. Therefore, the flatted third would be created by lowering the E one half step to E♭, the flatted fifth by lowering the G to G♭, and the flatted seventh by lowering the B to B♭.

The most prominent blues scale that's used to play over blues chord progressions employs all three of these flatted blue notes in this manner: C, E♭, F, F♯, G, B♭, C. Besides having the flatted third and the flatted seventh, this scale also uses both the flatted fifth (shown in the example as F♯, which is the same note as G♭) and the normal fifth, G, as consecutive notes.

Draw Bends

When you listen to great blues harmonica, most often you are hearing the artists play primarily draw notes, and many of those are bent draw notes. This is what is called playing cross harp, or playing in second position.

What Is a Draw Bend?

A draw bend is achieved by directing the air you draw through a hole so that it pulls both the draw reed and the blow reed simultaneously, creating a new note that is neither reed's natural tuning. The overall effect of a draw bend is always to pull the pitch of the note down.

On the C diatonic harmonica the 2 hole can be bent as far as a whole step below its natural note, moving from a G down to an F. You can also get the F♯, or half-step bend, by manipulating the airflow. That's three clean notes from a single draw hole. This is not easy to achieve and will require many hours to perfect, so don't give up. Being able to draw bend makes the difference between sounding like a grade-schooler or Charlie Musselwhite. Draw bends expand the range of the instrument tenfold.

HARP TIP

The Hohner XB-40 Extreme Bending Harmonica has note-bending capacity never seen on previous instruments. While normal diatonic harps can only be bent a half step or more on eight of the nineteen notes, the XB-40 allows every note on the instrument to be bent a whole step using normal bending technique, thanks to twenty extra reeds.

Playing a Draw Bend, Step by Step

When you're trying to get a bend, remember that it takes experimentation until you find the right "mouth" for it. Try going through these steps:

1. Using your correct embouchure for a single note, draw the 2 hole on your harmonica. Listen to its pure sound, nice and clean and clear, before you attempt to get your bend.

2. Take a moment to be aware of where in your mouth you have placed your tongue and how much air you are drawing to get that nice, clean, unbent sound.

3. Using the same amount of air pressure on the draw, try pulling the back of your tongue toward the back of your throat. This causes the air, even though it's drawn at roughly the same pressure, to move through a more constricted passageway and thus to enter the hole at a higher rate of speed, which will create more pressure on the reed and produce a change in the note. Usually these first bends you try sound awful and are nearly impossible to maintain, but don't get discouraged.

4. As you're practicing, be aware of your breath and how it changes as it is being redirected through your mouth. Changing your tongue's position will make it possible to find and learn just the right point and airflow you need to create the bend.

5. Practice this until you can get a full-step bend to the F note on this hole.

Eventually you will be able to get the full bend and the half-step bend and, if you are very good, all the semitones in between.

Every draw reed gets its bend from the same method, so once you have found it you won't forget it; you will only need to adjust it slightly for each reed that you can bend. The hardest part once you have the basic approach is not being satisfied until you can get the bend notes clean and clear.

HARMONICA HERO: RICK ESTRIN

Rick Estrin (b. 1949) is easily recognizable by his rich, fat harmonica sound, his magnificent bending technique, and his overall dexterity on the instrument. He is also known for his excellent and prolific songwriting. He has played with Muddy Waters and Buddy Guy and worked with Sam Lay, Eddie Taylor, Johnny Young, and John Littlejohn. Estrin formed the Nightcats in 1976 with guitarist Charlie Baty. During their early career, the Nightcats backed up a host of blues legends, including Big Mama Thornton, Albert Collins, John Lee Hooker, and Gatemouth Brown. Rick Estrin and the Nightcats are still going strong.

Exercises

A simple exercise you can try to get your bends in really good shape is to just practice them over and over again, seeing if you can find each individual tone that you can get with your bend.

FIGURE 2-3. DRAW BEND

Here's another exercise: play the 2 draw, then the 3 draw, and the 4 draw, bending each note as you go up the scale. You should try bending all the notes on your harmonica. You'll find that you can get many tones in between when you practice enough.

FIGURE 2-4. DRAW BEND EXERCISE GOING UP THE SCALE

More Advanced Techniques

These techniques might be familiar to your ear, but they're not easy to master. In fact, these sounds might be what drew you to the harmonica in the first place. The difficulty of mastering these techniques will vary depending on your mouth shape and size and your approach to playing.

Blow Bends

Blow bends are similar to draw bends, but they're a lot more difficult to play. The basic idea is the same as the draw bend, but it is executed using the blow rather than the draw. The approach is similar as well. It requires a lot of experimentation and then practice once you have found the right mouth and tongue positions. Blow bends also lead to overblows.

Overblows

An overblow is yet another additional note you can get out of your harmonica. While a blow bend vibrates both reeds simultaneously to produce the bend effect, an overblow jams one of the reeds while vibrating the other reed to create an overtone.

HARP TIP

Friction between your mouth and the harmonica will interfere with your technique. Be sure your lips are moist at all times when you're playing, and lick the parts of the harp your mouth will be touching, both before you play and periodically while you're playing for maximum mobility.

While draw bends and blow bends can only lower the pitch of a note, overblows have the effect of raising the note—by sounding an overtone of the reed pitch instead of the reed pitch itself. With overblows the effect of blowing through the hole at the right speed creates vibration in both the blow and the draw reed, creating an additional tone. Every note has several overtones above it. You can hear an example of how overtones occur by doing this exercise: while singing one constant note, move your mouth very slowly from a tight "oooooooh" sound to a wide open "aaaaaaaah" sound. As your mouth opens, you will hear the natural overtones of the note you're singing come in one at a time above the original pitch.

Overblows are an advanced technique that is hard to master, so don't be discouraged if you can't play one early in your harmonica career.

TAB: 7↑

FIGURE 2-5. BLOW BEND

Classic Riffs with Draw Bends

Once you have achieved a certain amount of control over your bends and have learned as many of them as you can find on your C harmonica, you will want to use these new tools to create "riffs." A riff is a series of notes that are often used as the building blocks of a song.

One classic riff that most people would recognize is the "Mannish Boy," or "Bad to the Bone," riff. This is a great example of how a musical idea, or phrase, is used to create a whole song. In fact, this riff is so complete that a harmonica alone is enough to play the song. This classic blues riff is one of the most common you'll hear in blues. It's famously played by McKinley Morganfield, better known as Muddy Waters.

FIGURE 2-6. CLASSIC RIFF WITH DRAW BEND 1

This riff is played by using:

1 draw—2 draw bend—1 draw—2 draw bend—2 draw unbent

This riff is often used in blues to punctuate the space that occurs between the vocals in a song. Typically the vocals and the harp riff would alternate in this way: counting each 4/4 measure as "1-and-2-and-3-and-4-and," the vocal line would be sung over counts "and-2-and-3" while the harmonica riff would be played over counts "and-4-and-1." So the overall effect would sound like this:

"Gypsy woman told my mother" (play riff)
"Before I was born" (play riff), and so on.

Here are some other classic blues riffs that feature draw bends:

FIGURE 2-7. CLASSIC RIFF WITH DRAW BEND 2

FIGURE 2-8. CLASSIC RIFF WITH DRAW BEND 3

Here is the classic "Fannie Mae" riff:

FIGURE 2-9. CLASSIC RIFF WITH DRAW BEND 4

Trills

A *trill* is defined as two notes played in a rapidly alternating manner. On the harmonica, a trill is created either by using your mouth to move between two holes or by moving the harmonica itself across two holes to create a continuous sound that plays two notes one after the other. Both methods of achieving this trill effect are valid. The idea is to get the notes to sound clearly and in the right rhythm.

Trills are one of the more dynamic riffs in harmonica playing. A trill can be clean or bent as the player wishes, and you know you're doing it well when it sounds clear and not too "breathy." For instance, play a trill on the 5-6 draw. Notice that bending the notes while playing the trill works effectively and creates a nice dynamic.

FIGURE 2-10. TRILLS

HARP TIP

The notation "4/4 time" is used in Western musical notation to specify how many beats are contained in each measure and which note value equals one beat. In a music score, the time signature appears at the beginning, as a time symbol or stacked numerals. Most music is in 4/4, also known as common time.

The following example is a little bit more advanced: it combines a trill, draw bends, and rhythm exercise all into one. The trill is noted with a squiggly line in the music notation.

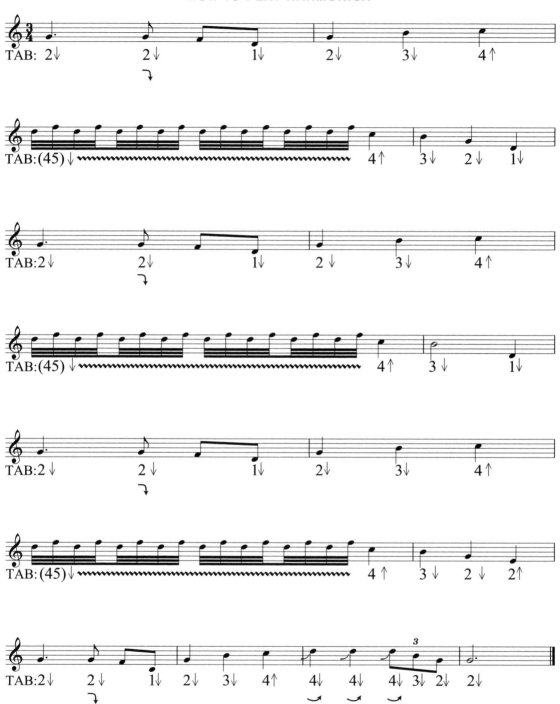

FIGURE 2-11. CLASSIC RIFF WITH DRAW BEND 5

With an arsenal that includes clean single notes and draw bends alone you should be able to play many of the great tried-and-true harmonica riffs.

Slurs

A *slur* is defined as a group of notes played together smoothly with one note flowing directly into the next, as opposed to articulating each note individually. On the harmonica slurs are often created when, instead of playing only the single notes that are part of the melody of the song, a player plays all the notes in between on the harp by passing over them quickly. It is an effective technique for adding tension to the song by creating a quick buildup to the next note.

What is important about playing a slur is that it sounds deliberate and that you don't spend too much time on any of the in-between notes. Otherwise it will sound sloppy, as though the player isn't in control of the instrument. This technique can be effective when soloing to add tension or to bring your solo to a resolution, as in the following example.

FIGURE 2-12. SLURS

Exercises for Playing Bends

Here's the most important thing to remember when trying to get your bends right—if they are not clear and in control, then you don't have it yet. Each note needs to sound correct—meaning that it's bent to exactly the right degree—and to accomplish this your breath needs to be right on target. Try to get every bend you can out of your harmonicas and develop them as you continue to learn and practice.

HARP TIP

The Bendometer Playing System uses a software program and a microphone connected to your computer to teach you how to play accurate bends. The program works like a tuner and shows you the notes you're playing on the computer screen. There is also an app version. Find out more at Harpsoft.com.

Try each bend going from the 1 hole to the 10 hole, and once you get one, you can keep trying to get the others. Your patience and practice will eventually reward you with a much bigger musical vocabulary.

HARMONICA HERO: BOB DYLAN

Bob Dylan (b. 1941) is the best-known singer-songwriter in contemporary modern music. He burst onto the music scene in the early 1960s with lyrics so powerful that he became the spokesperson for his generation for years. The harmonica has been an ever-present part of Dylan's performances, and the image of his harp held in a metal brace around his neck is burned into the minds of music fans everywhere. He has incorporated the harmonica into every album he has recorded, spanning the many different musical phases of his career. Dylan started out as a strong proponent of the first-position, major-key approach to harmonica, but once he moved to New York City and learned to play cross harp he leaned toward that style as well as sometimes playing in the relative minor. He is still active today as a songwriter, performer, and recording artist.

Exercise 1 for Playing Bent Notes

In this exercise we'll be hitting half-step bends on holes 1, 3, 4, and 5.

FIGURE 2-13. EXERCISE FOR PLAYING BENDS 1

Exercise 2 for Playing Bent Notes

It is extremely important that you get the 2-draw bend—it is a whole-step bend, and it must be clean every time for you to get the resolution of your cross-harp songs.

FIGURE 2-14. EXERCISE FOR PLAYING BENDS 2

Next, Chapter 3 looks at the rhythmic accompaniment that supports harmonica playing and how to interact with it.

Chapter 3

UNDERSTANDING RHYTHM

Rhythm is the pulse and the heartbeat of music. From the beginning of recorded history, man has been playing drums and other percussion instruments. In ancient tribal dances, the drums were what connected all the dancers in a common rhythm. Drums perform the same function today in a modern rock, jazz, or blues band—all the players sync up with the drummer and by doing so, all the players lock together into a common groove. How does the harmonica fit into the picture? Let's find out.

Counting

Even when there is no drummer playing, every piece of music has its own rhythm and its own *tempo*, a musical word that describes the speed at which a piece is played. When an ensemble of musicians is playing together, all the musicians know and are in agreement about what the rhythm and the tempo of the piece will be. When you're playing a piece of music by yourself, you'll still need to have the rhythm and the tempo of the music in mind to play it with the right feel.

The beat of a song defines its rhythm and pace. It's the centerpiece of the music, around which everything else is built. The *beat* of a piece of music is defined by its time signature, so 4/4 means four beats per measure (more on time signatures in the following section).

HARMONICA HERO: SONNY TERRY

Sonny Terry (1911–1986) was the most prominent blues harmonica player on the American folk music scene for over thirty years. He became known for crossing over from blues to folk music and blurring the lines between the two styles. He also introduced the innovation of using vocal sounds through his harmonica while playing, giving the instrument a unique sound. He was partially blinded from an accident as a young child, and then another accident at around age sixteen blinded him completely. Because he needed a career that took his handicap into account, Terry opted to take up singing blues and playing the harmonica, having been taught by his father. Terry recorded with folk luminaries Pete Seeger, Woody Guthrie, and Lead Belly.

Before a band begins a song, you'll often hear the bandleader or the drummer "count off" the time by saying "1-2-3-4" or something similar—this count is delivered at the exact speed the song will be played, and this alerts all the other musicians about what pace they'll be playing and also what the length of one measure is.

HARP TIP

There are hundreds of annual harmonica festivals around the United States and around the world every year where players and enthusiasts meet to revel in the instrument. These include the Spring Harp Fest in San Diego, the Buckeye Harmonica Festival in Columbus, Ohio, and the Atlantic Canada Harmonica Festival in Nova Scotia.

Besides counting the beats of a measure, when you're first learning about chord progressions, you might find yourself having to count the measures, or bars, as they go by to keep track of where you are. A chord progression is the series of chords that are played to accompany the melody of a song. For example, a very common chord progression in blues is the 12-bar blues progression, also called a 12-bar blues. Just like it sounds, a 12-bar blues takes twelve measures to play through the entire chord progression one time. If you're trying to count measures in a progression, the way to do it is to replace the "1" of the 1-2-3-4 beat count in each measure with the measure number instead, which would look like this for a 12-bar blues:

One-2-3-4	Two-2-3-4	Three-2-3-4	Four-2-3-4
Five-2-3-4	Six-2-3-4	Seven-2-3-4	Eight-2-3-4
Nine-2-3-4	Ten-2-3-4	Eleven-2-3-4	Twelve-2-3-4

HARP TIP

The Guinness World Record for the fastest harmonica player was established by Nicky Shane in California on September 8, 2005. The heavy-metal-style harmonica player astonished everyone by playing at the hair-on-fire speed of 285 beats per minute.

When you're first learning about rhythm and beats, you may find yourself spending a lot of time counting in your head—or even out loud—while you're playing to make sure you know where you are in the measure or in the chord progression. But as time goes by and you start to feel rhythm, beats, and progressions naturally you'll find that you don't have to count anymore because you'll know where you are by feel alone.

Mastering Rhythm When Playing in a Group

When you're playing by yourself, you're free to experiment and go wherever your imagination takes you. You can start, stop, and veer down any path you like—and you should, because following your impulses and going wherever your curiosity leads you is a great way to learn about music.

But when you're playing with other people, or "playing ensemble," that all changes. Now your common objective with the other musicians becomes to sound as good as possible as a unit. This means you have to suppress your natural impulse to play constantly and start thinking about what's going to make the group sound best. Generally this means allowing the musical focus to be either on the group as a unit or on one musician at a time, with the other musicians "comping" for him—*comping* being a jazz term that means playing what complements the lead musician's solo.

HARP TIP

Looking to interact with other harmonica players? Check out the many harmonica clubs that exist in practically every city. You can locate them by searching on Meetup.com or other social media sites. If there isn't already a harmonica group in your area, you can list yourself as someone who's interested in having one.

Comping for another musician includes *not* playing anything that distracts from what the soloist is doing, but rather playing notes, chords, or phrases that enhance what the soloist is playing and spurs him on to greater heights.

This section might as well be called "when *not* to play" because that's the real guiding factor in tasteful ensemble playing. Here are some of the basic rules:

- Don't play when the singer is singing, except during breaks in the vocals. A good way to practice this concept is to sing the song lyrics yourself and then fit harmonica phrases in the spaces between the vocal lines—this exercise automatically prevents you from playing over the vocals.
- Don't play when someone else is taking a solo, except for possibly comping as mentioned previously.
- Don't play when the opening or closing melodies are being stated (unless you're playing the exact melodies).
- Don't play if you haven't figured out the sound of the chord progression yet or if you get confused about where you are in the progression during a song. Wait to jump in when you get your bearings.

Remember, when you're playing music with other musicians, choosing *not* to play sometimes and purposely leaving empty space for the other players to occupy can be just as musical as playing. And when it's your turn to solo you'll appreciate it when your fellow musicians support you in these ways.

Advanced Tongue Techniques That Create Rhythm

You've already learned how to use your tongue to get single notes on the harmonica. But the tongue is capable of much more than that. It can also be used to create alternating chords and octaves, to create syncopated rhythms, and to alternate between single notes and chords.

Tongue techniques add depth and variety to your play, and effective use of advanced tongue techniques can signal the difference between being a good harp player and being a great one. As discussed earlier, basically tongue technique is just what it sounds like—using your tongue to block specific holes while allowing only the holes you want to get air. These techniques can help you track and create rhythm.

HARMONICA HERO: STEVIE WONDER

"Little" Stevie Wonder (b. 1950) burst upon the Motown music scene in 1963 with his album *Recorded Live: The 12-Year-Old Genius*. His first big hit was a harmonica solo from that album called "Fingertips—Part 2," which became a number one hit on the Billboard Hot 100 chart. As his career went on he became the leading voice of harmonica of his time in pop music. His signature chromatic harmonica style (with slide-in as the home position) has become one of the most widely imitated sounds on that instrument. His joyous harmonica solo on the 1968 hit "For Once in My Life" is a shining example of his buoyant and lyrical approach to melody. Wonder recorded "Alfie," an instrumental harmonica single in 1968, but Motown declined to release it, instead allowing another label to put it out with the artist listed as Eivets Rednow, a lightly disguised version of Wonder's name.

HARMONICA HERO: JUNIOR WELLS

Junior Wells (1934–1998) was best known for his swaggering bravado in performance and for carrying on the rich harmonica tradition of Little Walter and Sonny Boy Williamson II. He became commonly known as the Godfather of the Blues. His first major gig was with the Aces, featuring guitarists Louis and Dave Myers and drummer Fred Below. Wells joined Muddy Waters in 1952, filling the sudden void left by the departure of Little Walter. In the 1960s Wells teamed up with Buddy Guy to form a popular act that lasted many years. Wells also performed in later years with top rock artists, including the Rolling Stones and Van Morrison.

Try using the tongue-blocking method you already know to get a single note. Position your mouth as if to play a four-note chord using holes 1-2-3-4. Then use your tongue to block holes 1 through 3 and allow the air to move past your tongue as you play just the 4 hole. This will sound a single note. Try doing this exercise all the way up the harmonica. Then try blocking the other side, covering the three upper holes and allowing the lowest note in the group to sound. This technique works for both blow and draw notes.

Playing Octaves

This same tongue-blocking concept can be modified to get octaves as well. Octaves are often used to add strength to a given note by doubling it. In music the word *doubling* means using two voices to play the same note, phrase, or part.

Octaves are achieved on the harmonica by modifying the tongue-blocking technique used to play single notes. In this case the tongue is used to block the middle holes between the octave notes you're trying to play, allowing the air to pass on both sides of your tongue until you have two clean octave notes sounding on the harmonica simultaneously. Try it now by positioning your mouth as if to play the same four-note chord using holes 1-2-3-4 that you used previously for tongue blocking—but instead of blocking all but one hole, use your tongue to block holes 2 and 3, allowing the air to flow into holes 1 and 4. Again, this works with blow and draw notes. When done properly you should hear two clean C notes that are an octave apart.

Among the blow notes the octaves that are available to you occur between holes 1 and 4 (C), 2 and 5 (E), 3 and 6 (G), 4 and 7 (C), 5 and 8 (E), 6 and 9 (G), and 7 and 10 (C).

Among the draw notes the available octaves occur between holes 1 and 4 (D), 3 and 7 (B), 4 and 8 (D), 5 and 9 (F), and 6 and 10 (A). Note that the last four of these octaves require you to block three holes with your tongue, which is difficult even for experienced harp players, so they are shown more for your reference than as a suggested exercise.

Practice this octave technique until you can get a clean octave sound between the combinations of holes previously listed. This technique is a building block for learning the other advanced tongue-blocking techniques to follow.

HARP TIP

Can't get enough of harmonica music? Grab a harmonica ringtone for your phone! They come in all styles, from short phrases to full four-measure lines. Check out AudioSparx.com to find some harmonica ringtones.

Tongue Slapping

Tongue slapping is a technique that employs basic tongue blocking and adds the action of moving the tongue on and off of the comb to block and unblock holes in order to change the number of notes being played at one time.

You can try tongue slapping by playing one of your octaves and then moving your tongue off and on the middle holes that it's blocking. Notice that the sound shifts back and forth from the octave sound to the full chord sound.

Tongue Vamping

Tongue vamping combines the techniques of tongue blocking and tongue slapping to create a repeating rhythmic pattern of alternating single notes and chord sounds.

The idea of tongue vamping is to use a phrase or idea repetitively within the rhythm of a song, which has the effect of creating the sound of a single-note melody being accompanied by chords, all being played on one harmonica.

Following is an example of tongue vamping. This concept combines two techniques: playing an octave on your harmonica by blocking holes 2 and 3 while playing holes 1 and 4. First you'll hear all four holes, and then you'll hear holes 2 and 3 blocked so that you can hear the octave. By rhythmically lifting and replacing the tongue over holes 2 and 3 you create the vamp.

Examples:

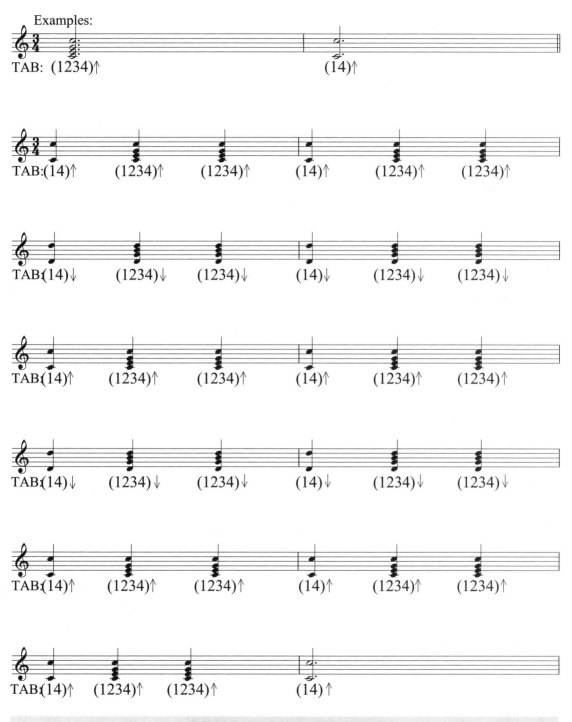

FIGURE 3-1. TONGUE VAMPING

Tongue Shuffle

In the examples of 4/4 time up to this point, the measures have been divided either into their individual four beats or into an "eighth-note feel," where each count of the measure gets two beats (counted "1-and-2-and-3-and-4-and").

A shuffle rhythm uses a different way of approaching 4/4 time. In this case each of the four beats in the measure is divided into three equal parts known as triplets. Each measure would be counted "1-and-a-2-and-a-3-and-a-4-and-a." The rhythm is then further refined by accenting just the first and last beat of each group of triplets, which looks like this:

1-and-**a**-**2**-and-**a**-**3**-and-**a**-**4**-and-**a** **1**-and-**a**-**2**-and-**a**-**3**-and-**a**-**4**-and-**a**

To *accent* means to play a beat or note more loudly than the beats or notes surrounding it, thereby emphasizing it. The overall effect is to create a kind of skipping rhythm that's quite driving and full of forward motion. In fact, some people like to say that it's easy to remember what a shuffle rhythm sounds like because it sounds just like its name: "shuffle-shuffle-shuffle-shuffle."

On harmonica, a tongue shuffle combines the techniques of tongue vamping, tongue slapping, octaves, and single notes to create a shuffle rhythm.

HARP TIP

Some great examples of the shuffle rhythm can be heard on songs such as "Key to the Highway," the Big Bill Broonzy/Charlie Segar song played often by Eric Clapton; "On the Road Again," by Canned Heat; and "Sweet Home Chicago," the Robert Johnson song played by Muddy Waters, Buddy Guy, Clapton, and practically every other blues artist.

HARMONICA HEROINE: CHRISTELLE BERTHON

Christelle Berthon is called the Harmonica Queen of *YouTube*—her page (www.youtube.com/user/christellester) has more than twenty-four million views! She was born in France and grew up studying the oboe. She later switched to harmonica and the rest is history. She is a master in a wide variety of genres, such as jazz, blues, and Celtic, and she is also famous for her ability to over-bend. Berthon has played with Jean-Jacques Milteau, Kenny Neal, Jason Ricci, Melody Gardot, and Charlie Musselwhite.

Here's a cool shuffle phrase you can try. It uses the shuffle rhythm described previously, but the phrase begins on the last triplet note of the previous measure, so the count will shift to look like this:

a-1-and-**a-2**-and-**a-3**-and-**a-4**-and

Then play each of the accented beats as follows:

a–1	2 draw
a	1-2-3-4 draw
2	1-2-3-4 blow
a	1-2-3-4 blow
3	1-2-3-4 draw
a	1-2-3-4 draw
4	2 blow

Articulation Syllables

If someone is speaking or singing in a sloppy or unintelligible way, it distracts from what he is trying to say. Harmonicas, like all musical instruments, are vessels used to express the feelings and ideas of the player. A great player is one who masters the ability to express those feelings and thoughts clearly through his instrument, without obvious technical errors, and a big step toward that goal is being able to play notes cleanly.

Creating rhythms also requires an ability to control the attack on the harp, so at this point it becomes more important for you to have a good understanding of how to create a sharp attack on your notes using articulation syllables. The word *attack* is used in music to describe how a note starts. It can start smoothly using just breath, or it can start suddenly. Articulation syllables are letter sounds such as *d* and *t* that you make with your mouth at the beginning of each note to release a concentrated amount of air to produce the hard attack. Using articulations such as *duh* and *tah* to create better-sounding notes will allow you to play more cleanly and is most important to playing well. The *t* sound is used for sudden blow notes. The *d* sound is used for sudden draw notes. To create the *d* sound with a draw requires you to block your mouth with the tip of your tongue and as you draw the air, release it by unblocking the airway, creating a *duh* sound while drawing breath.

FIGURE 3-2. ARTICULATION SYLLABLES

Simple Rhythms and Syncopated Rhythms

The word *syncopated* means the emphasizing of beats that are normally not the strong or accented beats in the rhythm you're playing. This is accomplished by accenting these weak beats.

For example, in 4/4 time where each measure has four beats, a simple rhythm would emphasize the first beat in each measure, like this:

1-2-3-4 **1**-2-3-4 **1**-2-3-4 **1**-2-3-4

Or it might emphasize all four beats equally. By contrast, a syncopated rhythm might accent the second and fourth beat of each measure, as is common in rock, blues, and country music, like this:

1-**2**-3-**4** 1-**2**-3-**4** 1-**2**-3-**4** 1-**2**-3-**4**

Another way to create syncopation is to add accents that fall between the beats of the measures, such as by accenting the first and fourth beats of each measure and then adding another accent on the half-beat (also known as the "and of the beat" because of the way it's counted) between the fourth and first beats, like this:

1-and-2-and-3-and-**4**-**and** **1**-and-2-and-3-and-**4**-**and**

Syncopated rhythms add tension and energy to music, making it sound more layered and interesting when that is what's called for. You normally wouldn't want to add syncopation to a song with a simple rhythm such as "Twinkle, Twinkle Little Star," a song that emphasizes all four beats of the measure equally, but if you were to experiment by adding the previous syncopated beat with the 4-and-1 accents you would find that the syncopated beat adds energy and drive to the song that wasn't there before, and makes the song sound very different.

The following examples illustrate the difference between simple rhythms and syncopated rhythms. The first example is a simple rhythm.

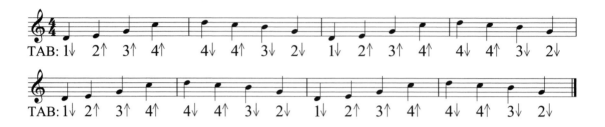

FIGURE 3-3. SIMPLE RHYTHMS

The following example is a syncopated rhythm.

FIGURE 3-4. SYNCOPATED RHYTHMS

HARP TIP

When you're practicing it's tempting to play all the things you can already play well, but if you want to expand your technique it's important to purposely take yourself out of your comfort zone by trying things you don't know how to play or aren't already good at playing. Overcoming these challenges will increase your confidence and your abilities.

Rhythmic Exercises

In the following rhythmic exercises you'll have the opportunity to combine many of the techniques you've learned up to this point—including playing single notes and chords, using syncopation, and playing rhythm—into phrases and "licks."

Practice these exercises often and the techniques will mesh and support one another, becoming new tools you can command.

HARP TIP

When traveling with your harmonicas, remember that they can show up on airport security checks. It's best if you announce that you have harmonicas before you put your bag through the X-ray machine.

Here's a rhythm exercise for you to try. This one involves going from chords to single notes and back to chords.

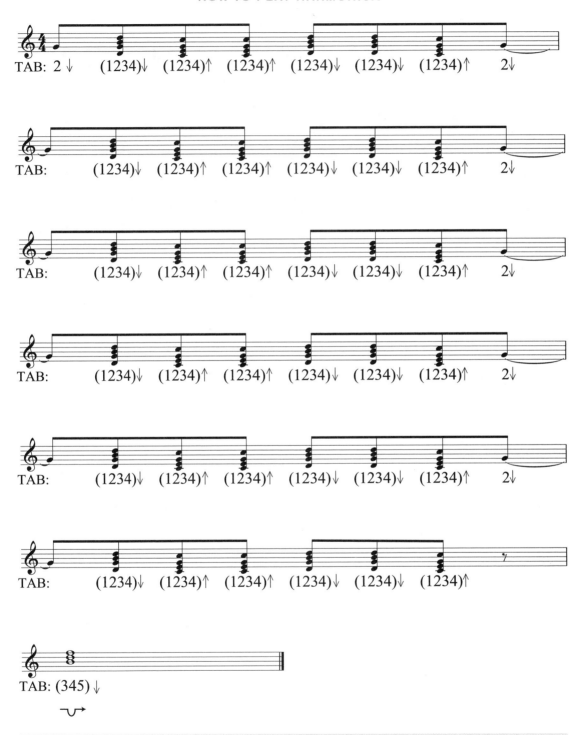

FIGURE 3-5. RHYTHM EXERCISE 1

Now try learning the harmonica riff demonstrated in the following two tablatures.

TAB: 2↓ 1↓ 2↑ 2↓ 1↓ 2↑ 2↓   1↓ 2↑ 2↓ 1↓ 2↑ 2↓   1↓ 2↑ 2↓ 1↓ 2↑ 2↓

FIGURE 3-6. RHYTHM EXERCISE 2—BLUES SHUFFLE

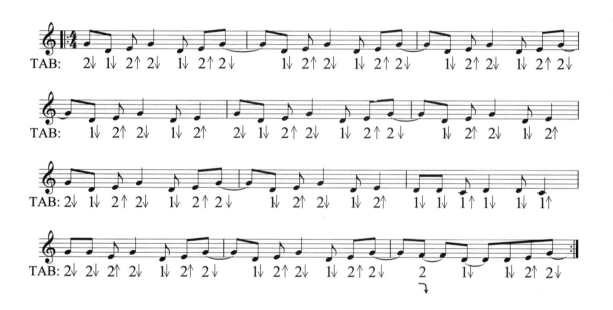

TAB: 2↓ 1↓ 2↑ 2↓ 1↓ 2↑ 2↓   1↓ 2↑ 2↓ 1↓ 2↑ 2↓   1↓ 2↑ 2↓ 1↓ 2↑ 2↓

TAB: 1↓ 2↑ 2↓ 1↓ 2↑   2↓ 1↓ 2↑ 2↓ 1↓ 2↑ 2↓   1↓ 2↑ 2↓ 1↓ 2↑

TAB: 2↓ 1↓ 2↑ 2↓ 1↓ 2↑ 2↓   1↓ 2↑ 2↓ 1↓ 2↑   1↓ 1↓ 1↑ 1↓ 1↓ 1↑

TAB: 2↓ 2↓ 2↑ 2↓ 1↓ 2↑ 2↓   1↓ 2↑ 2↓ 1↓ 2↑ 2↓   2   1↓   1↓ 2↑ 2↓
                                                   ↓

FIGURE 3-7. RHYTHM EXERCISE 3—BLUES SHUFFLE

Melody and Chording Together

Combining melody and chords into one piece of music comes naturally for the harmonica. The design of the instrument is set up to facilitate playing chords on the lower end while making it easy to play scales on the upper end. This technique is also one of the most interesting and dynamic approaches to playing the harmonica, allowing the instrument to function in the role of stand-alone accompaniment or as a powerful rhythmic and solo voice in a band.

HARMONICA HERO: NEIL YOUNG

Neil Young (b. 1945) has been a fixture on the music scene since the early 1960s. He first became widely known as a member of the band Buffalo Springfield, but it was after he left that group that his career really took off. Young released a series of extremely popular albums as a solo artist and later hooked up with Crosby, Stills, and Nash to form one of the supergroups of the 1970s. Young has always been a strong proponent of the harmonica, to the point that it's a trademark of the sound he's known for. He has featured it on many of his best-known songs including "Heart of Gold," "Helpless," "After the Gold Rush," "My My, Hey Hey," and "Rockin' in the Free World." The introductory harp melody to "Heart of Gold" is one of the best-known harmonica lines in modern music. Young also played harmonica on the track "Furry Sings the Blues" on Joni Mitchell's popular 1976 album *Hejira*. Young popularized the first-position, major-key folk music approach to harmonica, and his harp parts are tabbed and studied often by those learning the instrument. He is still active on the music scene today.

Here's an example of melody and chording in the same song:

FIGURE 3-8. MELODY AND CHORDING TOGETHER

Arpeggios

You'll recall from Chapter 1 that a chord is comprised of three or more notes played at the same time. An *arpeggio* is another way of playing a chord—but rather than playing all the notes at once, an "arpeggiated" chord is produced by playing the notes in the chord one at a time in sequential order. Arpeggios can be played in either ascending or descending order of notes, meaning you can start with the lowest note and move up through the notes of the chord or you can start with the highest note and move down. You can play an example of a series of C major triad arpeggios simply by blowing holes 1 through 10 one at a time.

FIGURE 3-9. ARPEGGIO

HARMONICA HERO: GEORGE "HARMONICA" SMITH

George "Harmonica" Smith (1924–1983), aka Little George Smith, Harmonica King, and Little Walter Junior, was a prominent blues singer and harmonica player who emerged on the scene in the 1940s. He was considered the leading chromatic harp player among the blues players of the time and a leading proponent of using octave melodies in his solos. He is also known as one of the earliest experimenters of playing the harmonica through an amplified sound system, the first one of which he extracted from a film projector at the movie theater where he worked. He played with Otis Rush, Muddy Waters, the Myers brothers (Louis and Dave), Champion Jack Dupree, and Little Willie John.

Chapter 4

PLAYING IN DIFFERENT KEY POSITIONS

Up until now the main focus of your training has been playing the harmonica in first position, with its simple major key sound. While that sound is charming and has many uses, it is only part of the diatonic harmonica's capability. Learning to play in other positions greatly expands the types of chord sounds and chord progressions you can play over. Most people first become interested in the harmonica from hearing it played in second position or cross harp. In this chapter you'll learn the all-important second and third positions on the harmonica.

Determining Which Harp to Play Based on a Song's Key

Because diatonic harmonicas are designed to be centered on one major scale, you can't use the same instrument to play in every key like you can with a chromatic harmonica. This means two things:

1. You'll eventually need to have more than one harmonica—in fact, more like seven harmonicas—if you want to have the ability to play in many different keys with other musicians.
2. You'll need to know which harmonica to select to play in any given key.

Choosing the right harmonica when playing with others depends on both the song you want to play and the style in which you choose to play it. A folk-style or traditional song would require you to play a basic melody in the same key as the harmonica, so you would choose a harp that's in the same key as the song you want to play.

HARP TIP

Matthias Hohner, a German clockmaker, turned his full attention to the manufacturing of harmonicas in 1857, producing a total of 650 instruments that year. Thirty years later the Hohner company was producing over a million harmonicas per year, and today they make dozens of different models of harps in addition to other types of musical instruments.

HARMONICA HEROINE: BIG MAMA THORNTON

Big Mama Thornton (1926–1984) was a prominent blues singer, drummer, and harmonica player known for her gritty and energetic vocal style. In addition, she was the first to record two blues songs that made a huge impact on the American music scene. The first was "Hound Dog," released in 1953, which was a number one hit on the Billboard charts for seven weeks and was later famously covered by Elvis Presley in 1956. The other was "Ball and Chain," which she wrote and recorded in 1961 and which went on to become an enormous hit for singer Janis Joplin. She also played with many other blues luminaries including Lightnin' Hopkins, Muddy Waters, Junior Parker, Johnny Otis, James Cotton, and Otis Spann.

The term *position* refers to where on the harmonica the *tonic* (the first note of the scale of the key the song is in) is for the song you'll be playing. In other words, the note where you begin to play on the harmonica is what signifies the position you're playing in. For most players, the useful positions are the first, second, and third positions, and those are the ones that are discussed here.

First Position

Many basic tunes are in the key of C and are meant to be played using *straight harp*, or first position. First position is the natural tuning of the harmonica and is played mainly using the blow notes of the harp beginning with the 1 hole as the tonic or key of the song. (The 1 hole and the 4, 7, and 10 holes are the same note but one octave apart, so those could be starting notes too.)

Typically first-position songs are folk songs or traditional songs associated with the harmonica like "Home on the Range" or "On Top of Old Smokey." These melodies will often be played using the second octave note (4-hole blow) as the starting point to allow room for movement up and down the pitch range of the instrument.

4 5 6 7 Blow

FIGURE 4-1. FIRST POSITION ON HARMONICA

First-Position Licks

To play first position on the harmonica is to play in the key in which the harmonica was built. In this case, you'll be playing in the key of C using a C harmonica. First position is when you play mainly the blow notes of the harmonica.

TAB: 4↑ 4↑   4↑ 3↑ 5↑ 5↑ 5↑ 4↑ 4↑ 5↑ 6↑   6↑ 5↓ 5↑ 4↓

FIGURE 4-2. FIRST-POSITION LICKS

Second Position, or Cross Harp

Second position, also known as cross harp, begins on the 2-hole draw as the tonic or key of the song and builds from there using mainly draw notes. A blues song or rock-and-roll song would most likely require you to play in second position. For that position, you must choose a harp tuned to the key three notes above the key of the song. For example, for a song in the key of G you would select a C harmonica and then play in second position. Here's a quick reference about the correct harp for the key when playing cross harp:

C	D	E	F	G	A	B	harp
G	A	B	C	D	E	F♯	key

This would be the position for playing most blues songs that are in a major key. Be aware that second position relies heavily on the ability to bend notes to fill out the scale of the song.

2 3 4 5 6 Draw

FIGURE 4-3. SECOND POSITION ON HARMONICA

Second-Position Licks

In order to play cross harp, or second position, on the harmonica, your tonic note is always the 2 draw. On the C harmonica, in this case, it would be the key of G. Cross harp depends on mainly playing draw notes. So if the band is playing a blues in G, you should be playing cross harp on a C harp.

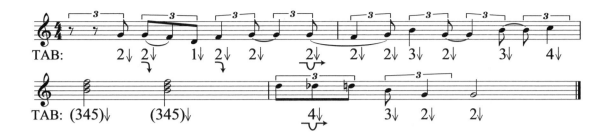

FIGURE 4-4. SECOND-POSITION LICKS

HARP TIP

Players who only practice second position often find it difficult to play any minor-key songs and will hit notes in a major scale that don't fit into the minor key chord progression. They will also believe that they can't play many songs because they "don't have the right key" harmonica. If you only practice one position, that is all you will be able to play, and you will be missing out on a lot of fun and growth as a musician.

The reason shifting to second position to play a blues scale in another key works is that the resulting scale has a flatted seven rather than the not-bluesy-sounding-at-all natural seven of a major scale. For example, on the C harmonica when you shift to second position and start playing in the key of G, the seventh note of the G scale naturally becomes an F, because F is part of the C scale, while F♯ would be the seventh note of a G major scale.

Third Position

Before talking about playing in third position, it's useful to look at the difference between a major scale and a minor scale. You're already familiar with the C major scale, which is:

$$C, D, E, F, G, A, B, C$$

The *natural minor* scale, which is the most common minor scale, has flatted third, sixth, and seventh notes. Therefore the C minor scale looks like this:

$$C, D, \textbf{E}\flat, F, G, \textbf{A}\flat, \textbf{B}\flat, C$$

Note that it's primarily the flatted third and the flatted seventh that give the minor scale its characteristic sound, and these notes are common to all minor scales.

HARMONICA HERO: BRUCE SPRINGSTEEN

Bruce Springsteen (b. 1949) has won an astonishing twenty Grammy awards and has sold millions of albums. The harmonica has been an integral part of Springsteen's recordings and performances since the beginning of his career, and in many ways he has carried on the Woody Guthrie tradition of the American singer/songwriter/harmonica-playing guitarist. He has played the harmonica on every recording and in every concert, especially featuring the instrument on his acoustic albums including *Nebraska* and *The Ghost of Tom Joad*. But even while carrying this traditional torch Springsteen has also forged new paths on the harmonica, incorporating it into top songs in the loud, electric rock genre in a prominent way on songs including "Thunder Road" from the *Born to Run* album, "The Promised Land" from the *Darkness on the Edge of Town* album, and "The River" from *The River* album. He is still recording and touring today.

HARP TIP

Modes are classical scales that grew out of ancient Greek music. They are centered on the notes of a C major scale, and each of the seven modes uses the same consecutive notes of that C major scale—but each mode begins on a different note of that scale. This means that in each mode the half steps and whole steps fall in different places, which is what gives each mode its unique sound.

Third position, also known as draw harp, is used to play most minor-key blues, and it begins on the 4 draw as the tonic, or key, of the song. This position enables you to play a minor scale known as the Dorian mode, which has a flatted third and a flatted seventh (but no flatted sixth as in the natural minor). Once again, you would need a harmonica that's in a different key than the key of the song. For example, if a song is in D minor you would again use the C harmonica, but this time you would play in third position.

Here's a quick reference about the correct harp for the minor key when playing in third position:

C	D	E	F	G	A	B	harp played in third position
Dm	Em	F♯m	Gm	Am	Bm	D♭m	minor key

As with second position, you will need to be able to bend notes to be able to have a full range of additional notes to play, but mostly you will play on the 4, 5, 6, and 7 holes.

4 5 6 7 Draw

FIGURE 4-5. THIRD POSITION ON HARMONICA

Third-Position Licks

In order to play third position on the harmonica, the 4, 5, 6, and 7 holes draw will allow you to play in a minor key. In the case of the C harmonica this would be D minor. If the band is playing in D minor and you wish to play along on your C harp, you would use third position, or holes 4, 5, 6, and 7 draw.

FIGURE 4-6. THIRD-POSITION LICKS

HARMONICA HEROINE: STACIE COLLINS

Stacie Collins is a high-energy singer-songwriter and harmonica performer. She was born in Muskogee, Oklahoma, and later moved to Bakersfield, California, and then Nashville, Tennessee. She plays in the style of Chicago blues greats Little Walter and James Cotton. She tours frequently and has released five records on her own label.

HARMONICA HERO: NORTON BUFFALO

Norton Buffalo (1951–2009) was a versatile harmonica player who was equally comfortable playing in the blues, rock, jazz, country, and R & B idioms. After playing with Commander Cody he joined the Steve Miller Band, and he remained the band's harmonica player for over twenty years, from the mid-1970s to the late 1990s. He also appeared as a studio musician on albums by Johnny Cash, Bonnie Raitt, and the Doobie Brothers. In the late 1980s he teamed up with blues slide guitarist Roy Rogers to form a duet act. Following that he formed his band the Knockouts, which recorded and performed for many years.

It's important to know that whichever position you play in you will need to be aware of the key of the song you are playing. From picking the right harmonica for the job to knowing whether you're playing in a major or a minor key and which notes are in the scale of that key, giving your playing this level of attention will improve your ability to play harmonica solos that make sense over the chord progressions you're working with. In addition, being aware of some of these simple rules of music theory will help you communicate with other musicians.

More Positions

There are actually, technically speaking, twelve possible positions on the diatonic harmonica because it is technically possible—through the use of bending, blow bends, and overblows—to play all twelve notes of the chromatic scale on a diatonic harp. But this is very difficult and rarely done.

The other two positions that are commonly used are fourth position and fifth position. *Fourth position* begins on the 6 draw and enables you to play a natural minor scale in A when played on a C diatonic harmonica. You'll recall from the previous sections that the natural minor scale is the one with a flatted third, sixth, and seventh.

Fifth position begins on the 5 blow and enables you to play another type of minor scale known as the Phrygian mode, which has a flatted second in addition to a flatted sixth and seventh.

HARMONICA HERO: PAUL OSCHER

Paul Oscher (b. 1950) wasn't hard to spot when he rose to prominence as the harmonica player for the Muddy Waters Blues Band—he was the only white musician in the band, or in any other major blues band of the time. Oscher broke the color barrier through his dedication to blues music and his skills as an accomplished harmonica player, guitarist, and singer. He first started performing on harmonica at age fifteen, and by age eighteen he was selected by Muddy Waters to become the harp player in his band, one of the top blues acts in the world. Oscher played with Waters from the late 1960s to the early 1970s, and from there went on to play with an astonishing array of top blues artists including Otis Spann, Johnny Copeland, Luther Johnson, Johnny Young, Big Mama Thornton, Buddy Guy, John Lee Hooker, and T-Bone Walker. Oscher is still an active artist on the blues scene today.

Playing harmonica in the various positions is a huge boost to understanding the complexities of the instrument. Eventually you'll grasp how all the notes on the harp and the bends and overblows that are available on each note fit together into the marvelous puzzle that is the diatonic harmonica.

Chapter 5

SONGS YOU CAN
PLAY IN
FIRST POSITION

The great thing about a harmonica is that you can start playing songs right off the bat with only a little know-how. You'll get nice-sounding chords anywhere up and down the ten holes of the diatonic harmonica, whether blowing or drawing the notes, and the unbent single notes you pick out also fit right into the scale. Now it's time to play a few real tunes to see how you're progressing.

Playing Melody

A *melody* is defined as a succession of single notes assembled to form a purposeful sequence. What's the purpose? As a musician your job is to convey the emotion of your melody with expressive playing. The way you do that is to focus emotion into your playing while you're doing it. This means that you don't just play one note after another and congratulate yourself when you make it to the end—you listen to and interpret what the melody conveys to you emotionally, and then you put that feeling back into your playing when you play the melody to pass the emotional content along to the listener. Even someone who isn't a musician can tell the difference between a song played mechanically and one played with feeling.

The melody is the focal point of a song or piece of music. In vocal music, the lyrics are sung to the melody line, and in instrumental music the melody is placed prominently above the accompaniment in volume. Whichever type of music you play on the harmonica, just be sure that you let your passion for the instrument shine through!

HARP TIP

Coughing can be a problem when you're playing the harmonica. Before a performance it might be useful to coat your throat, like a singer sometimes does, using cough lozenges. This will help to prevent coughing onstage and can also help reduce the effects of smoke in the venue if there is any.

Well-Known Folk Melodies You Can Play

Folk songs are by definition songs that have been passed on from generation to generation, which is why they're so deeply embedded in your consciousness. They're songs you've heard ever since you were a child, and songs that you'll probably sing to your own children. Elegant in their simplicity, folk songs employ few tricks or devices to get their point across, but rather communicate their well-worn messages with simple, memorable melodies.

HARMONICA HERO: CHARLIE MUSSELWHITE

Charlie Musselwhite (b. 1944), along with Paul Butterfield, is credited with making the blues crossover into the much larger rock audiences of the 1960s. As a teenager growing up in Memphis, he played with blues guitarist Furry Lewis. In 1962 he moved to Chicago, where he became a fixture in blues clubs, playing with Little Walter, Howlin' Wolf, and Muddy Waters. For years he also was the harmonica player for guitarist Big Joe Williams, replacing Sonny Boy Williamson I. Musselwhite also played with John Lee Hooker, Big Walter Horton, Johnny Young, Floyd Jones, and Robert Nighthawk. Musselwhite eventually settled in the San Francisco area, where he performed with a who's who of the top Bay Area guitarists, including Harvey Mandel, Louis Myers, and Robben Ford. Musselwhite is still an active recording artist and performer today.

Here are five classic folk melodies to build your repertoire of major-key songs played in first position.

"Simple Gifts"

The first melody, "Simple Gifts," is an old Shaker hymn that expresses humility, faith, and satisfaction with life.

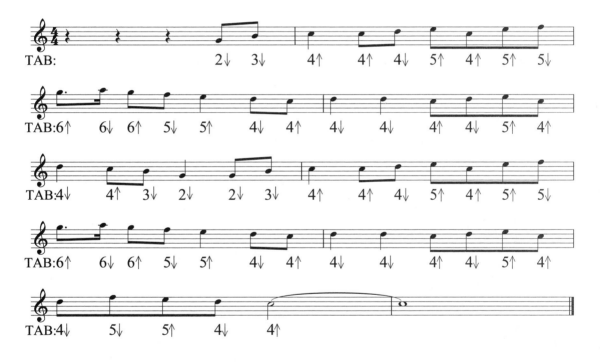

FIGURE 5-1. "SIMPLE GIFTS"

"Tom Dooley"

The second melody, "Tom Dooley," is an American folk song.

FIGURE 5-2. "TOM DOOLEY"

"Frankie and Johnnie"

The third melody, "Frankie and Johnnie," is another American folk song.

FIGURE 5-3. "FRANKIE AND JOHNNIE"

"On Top of Old Smokey"

The fourth melody, "On Top of Old Smokey," is another classic American folk song. It's generally sung with mirth by children ("On Top of Spaghetti").

FIGURE 5-4. "ON TOP OF OLD SMOKEY"

"Bill Bailey"

Finally, our fifth melody, "Bill Bailey," is a comical American folk song.

FIGURE 5-5. "BILL BAILEY"

HARMONICA HERO: MAGIC DICK

Magic Dick (b. 1945) is best known for his role as harmonica player in the J. Geils Band. In that context and throughout his career Dick has been a force for the modernization of the sound and the role of the harmonica in contemporary music. In 1968 he met John Geils and Danny Klein, and together with them he became a founding member of the J. Geils Blues Band in 1968. The band was together for twelve years and had a highly successful career of recording and performing. Dick has played harmonica as a sideman for Debbie Harry, Patty Smyth, and the Del Fuegos, among others. He also went on to form a new group, Bluestime, with longtime band member J. Geils. He continues to perform today.

Often you will find that a single note can be replaced by a chord or an octave to add depth, as on a song like "Simple Gifts." Once you can play these melodies with clean single notes, try playing them with chord melodies or using occasional octave notes played at the same time, and see how they sound.

Chord Melodies

Once you have played these melodies as single-note pieces try playing them with chords. *Chord melodies* are created by playing the notes above and below the main melody note to create the chords, and they sound like a three-part harmony. You can alternate between the single and chordal notes to create a richer sound.

Dropping chords and octaves into your single-note melodies feels natural when you hear it, but it can be a little tricky to decide exactly where to use these effects. This is always the case when beginning to play, but it becomes second nature after just a little practice. Start by playing the whole song through twice, first using only single notes and then using chords and octaves to create a dramatic build.

HARP TIP

The *country scale* is a variation of the major scale that's often used in country and folk music for its natural bouncy rhythm. It's played by selecting the first, second, third, fifth, sixth, and eighth (octave) notes of the major scale. The scale is also known as a major pentatonic scale.

Exercises for First-Position Play

Following are three exercises that will improve and refine your first-position play.

Breathing Exercise

First try a breathing exercise. More than any other position, first position demands that you be economical with your air because you're playing mainly blow notes. Try this: switch back and forth between playing a couple of single notes and then a chord. Make sure you're getting a full-sounding volume, but then focus on using the least amount of air pressure possible to maintain that volume. You'll realize how much excess air you normally use and how much longer you can play on the same breath if you're breathing from your diaphragm and conserving air.

Tongue-Slapping Exercise

This five-step tongue-slapping exercise will rapidly increase the accuracy of your tongue-slapping skills.

1. Using holes 4-5-6-7, play a *single note* on hole 7 blow while tongue-blocking holes 4, 5, and 6.
2. Switch to playing the *octave* holes 4 and 7 blow while tongue-blocking holes 5 and 6.
3. Play the *whole chord* 4-5-6-7 blow.
4. Switch back to playing the *octave* holes 4 and 7 blow while tongue-blocking holes 5 and 6.
5. Play the *single note* on hole 7 blow while tongue-blocking holes 4, 5, and 6.

Start slowly with each step until you can move from one to another cleanly, and then start speeding the exercise up.

HARMONICA HEROINE: ANNIE RAINES

Annie Raines (b. 1969) stands out in the world of blues harmonica for one reason besides her formidable talent—she was one of the first women to rise up to the rank of highly respected blues harmonica player. After studying the Chicago blues harp masters, she made her own pilgrimage to Chicago, where she played with James Cotton, Louis Myers, and Pinetop Perkins. She also has played with blues guitarist Susan Tedeschi, Rory Block, and John Sebastian. In 1993 she met blues guitarist Paul Rishell, and the two of them continue to record and perform together to this day.

HARMONICA HERO: PAUL BUTTERFIELD

Paul Butterfield (1942–1987) would be considered one of the greatest blues harmonica players of all time under any circumstances, but his case is made all the more special by the fact that he was the first white blues harp player to develop his own signature sound on the instrument and to have it considered legitimate by the black blues community. What's more, Butterfield's blazing harmonica style became a window through which large audiences of white listeners became attracted to blues music during the 1960s and 1970s, listeners who subsequently went on to explore the other icons of blues because of the rich experience they'd had listening to him. Butterfield's most important albums were *The Paul Butterfield Blues Band* (1965), *East-West* (1966), and *The Resurrection of Pigboy Crabshaw* (1967). He died of a drug overdose in Hollywood, California in 1987.

Octave-Jumping Exercise

Finally, here is an octave-jumping exercise. Try this series of notes:

6 blow—5 blow—4 blow—7 blow

The skill you're developing here is the octave jump from 4 blow to 7 blow. If you're not hitting the 7 blow cleanly when you jump, listen for whether it's the note above or the note below that's creeping in, and adjust the amount of your shift accordingly. You can also play this exercise using holes 3-2-1-4 and using holes 9-8-7-10.

HARMONICA HERO: TOOTS THIELEMANS

Toots Thielemans (1922–2016) is the unrivalled master of jazz chromatic harmonica. Many people have mistaken his harmonica tracks for a brilliant jazz saxophonist with unlimited technique, because the complexity and dexterity he brought to the chromatic harmonica was unheard of before his time. Thielemans was born in Belgium but eventually moved to the United States. Over the years Thielemans recorded and performed with the top names in jazz, including Bill Evans, Oscar Peterson, Ella Fitzgerald, Dizzy Gillespie, and Jaco Pastorius. He was also active on the Brazilian music scene, playing with Milton Nascimento, Gilberto Gil, and Luiz Bonfá.

Beautiful Is Better Than Loud!

When playing in first position, most of what you will play are blow notes and chords. Blowing requires that you economize with your breath so that you don't run out of air in the middle of a place where you should be playing. If you tend to blow as hard as you can, two things will happen: first, you will make the harp sound forced and distorted, and second, you will blow out the reeds. This means that either the reed can become permanently stuck or, much worse, go out of tune. If you don't notice that you have an out-of-tune reed, it can be disastrous during play, not to mention expensive to replace.

The better approach to playing first position is to get the sound you want using the least amount of effort necessary. Notes played cleanly and with good breath control sound a lot better than loud, out-of-tune, or forced notes. The emphasis on clear, clean notes rather than loud ones is important because if you are unplugged, there are a lot of instruments that you simply cannot compete with for volume. This will make you want to play as loud as you can, and that will lead to some poor-sounding harp playing.

If you are amplified, it is best to let the amp do the loud part while you just play it cool and stay focused on your clear playing. Let your amp create a desirable distorted sound, rather than distorting the sound of your harp out of fear of not being heard.

Lastly, you might find that on a song that has been played with a lot of volume and energy from the beginning, when it's time for the harmonica solo there's an opportunity for you to step up and play a soft, pretty melody to create contrast.

In today's music there's often a lot of pressure to be loud, and it can seem hard to compete against that trend when loudness is commonly equated with excitement. But just as you wouldn't want to eat the same food every day, hearing music at just one volume gets boring pretty quickly, and playing music at one volume only limits the emotional palette you have to work with.

HARMONICA HERO: BOB HITE

As lead singer and harmonica player of Canned Heat from 1965 to 1981, Bob Hite was one of the most prominent harmonica players of the 1960s and 1970s. Known as "The Bear" for his large stature, Hite was a masterful diatonic harmonica player whose syncopated rhythms percolated over Canned Heat's signature boogie beat. The infectious energy the band created with their blend of blues and rock drew the interest of huge audiences to harmonica-driven blues. Hite died of a heart attack during a performance in 1981.

Playing by Ear in First Position

Playing by ear (also called picking out melodies) is the skill of being able to hear a melody, a song, or any piece of music and then being able to play it. Some people can hear a song just once and have the uncanny ability to play it immediately. For others it takes listening to a song ten times before they're able to reproduce it. If you fall into the latter group you're in the majority, so don't worry. Playing by ear is a skill that can be acquired with practice.

There are two components to playing by ear:

1. The first is being able to listen to a song and remember what you heard.
2. The second is being able to find and play the notes you remember on your harmonica.

If you have a problem listening to a note and then reproducing it on your instrument, ear training will help you. Ear training is a series of exercises that teach you this skill. You can find courses online (such as Adam Gussow's instructional available on *YouTube*) that you can use to train your ear and develop this ability.

Play with Confidence

Part of playing any instrument is having confidence in your ability. This doesn't apply only when you're playing in front of an audience—confidence is even needed to play for just one other person. What's the source of this confidence? It comes from the knowledge that you've practiced enough that when you intend to play a phrase or song you know it will come out the way you intend.

No one wants to believe that they will be scared to play when the time comes, but in truth most people are, especially until they have done it a bunch of times. Even professional players have moments of nervousness before a performance. Maintaining your focus and confidence will go a long way toward making it easier to eliminate this nervousness and play for people.

HARP TIP

Harmonica competitions provide an outlet for the gunslingers among you. At these competitions you stand up at a microphone and you have three to six minutes to prove to the judges that you've got it. The big competitions include the annual National Harmonica League in England and the Asia-Pacific Harmonica Festival Harmonica Competition.

Chapter 7 will help you build confidence by teaching you how to practice effectively and set up your own practice schedule.

Chapter 6

IMPROVISATION

Many times when you see a lead guitarist or a blues harmonica player taking a solo in a live show, you're watching improvisation in action. The soloist steps forward and begins to play with no road map to guide her, allowing herself to be swept along by the rhythm and the chord progression until, in a stream of consciousness, a flurry of inspired notes emerges from her instrument. Even her band isn't sure what she might play next—this is the unpredictable beauty of improvisation. In this chapter, you will learn the basics of improvising without a net.

What Is Improvisation?

Improvisation is the spontaneous creation of music in the immediate moment, played without any written music or notation for guidance. Like forces of nature coming together, improvising musicians collide and bounce off each other, create force fields that propel each other, twist and turn and lead each other on a wild, unpredictable ride. The result is music that's being born before your very eyes, and it's a one-time experience that's never to be repeated. If your goal is to be here now and live in the moment, improvisation is for you!

Although improvised music is being created at the moment it's played, it often comes off sounding very organized. Great improvisation between musicians can come out sounding as complete and perfect as a painstakingly composed piece of music, where the different parts intertwine and build on each other to develop themes and variations between instruments that sound carefully planned and mapped out. The fact that such an illusion is possible shows you that real composition is taking place during improvisation. When you solo, you're composing music on the spot. There's even a saying that's common among jazz players: "Improvisation is composing speeded up, while composing is improvisation slowed down."

HARP TIP

Studying the harmonica solos of great players and copying them is an excellent way to improve your playing and broaden your musical knowledge. Try breaking down the solos into manageable phrases and playing them slowly until you can play each one—then string them together into the solo and speed up the tempo gradually.

HARMONICA HERO: SUGAR BLUE

Sugar Blue (b. 1949) is one of the most skilled and versatile instrumentalists playing harmonica today. His harp style blends jazz and blues influences propelled by his excellent technique and virtuosity on the instrument. Blue grew up in the environment of the famous Apollo Theater in Harlem, where his mother was a performer. He learned harmonica as a child and was doing recording sessions by the time he was twenty-five. Blue met Mick Jagger of the Rolling Stones while living in Paris in 1976. His well-known eighteen-note riff that opens the Rolling Stones track "Miss You" became one of the most prominent harmonica riffs in rock. Blue went on to play with Junior Wells, Carey Bell, James Cotton and Big Walter Horton, and Willie Dixon. He also played with jazz great Stan Getz, and in 1985 was awarded a Grammy for his work on a live jazz album from the Montreux Jazz Festival.

Being a great musician doesn't automatically mean you can improvise. Many highly trained classical players are not good improvisers because they've been trained their whole careers to read music and play whatever is put in front of them. When *nothing* is put in front of them they don't know what they're supposed to do.

Improvisation requires taking all the techniques and instincts you have developed as a musician and using them to navigate through the unknown, like a pathfinder riding a well-equipped wagon through uncharted territory. You don't know where you're going to end up, but you know you have the skills to get you there.

Components of Improvisation

There are many ways you can participate during ensemble improvisation. Each approach adds a different facet to the sound, and each requires a distinct set of skills on the part of the player.

Playing a Solo

Playing a solo is the first thing most people think of when they think of improvisation, because the person taking the solo is always the featured musician at the moment she is soloing, while the other musicians are taking a supporting role. In simple terms, improvising a solo consists of listening to the rhythm and the chord progression that are being played by the band and creating on-the-spot melody lines over those sounds. Improvised solos are scale-driven, meaning that the soloist must first know what key and what types of scales fit over the chord changes in order to improvise over those changes using notes that are appropriate.

HARMONICA HERO: JAMES COTTON

James Cotton (1935–2017) was a fixture on the blues harmonica scene for more than sixty years. He was a crowd-pleaser known for his powerful and energetic performances. Before he was ten years old he was taken under the wing—and into the house—of Sonny Boy Williamson II, who became his teacher and mentor. Cotton's first major gig was playing with Howlin' Wolf for four years beginning in 1950. In 1954 Cotton replaced Little Walter as the harmonica player for Muddy Waters and stayed with him until 1966. Then in 1967 Cotton became the leader of his own band, the James Cotton Blues Band. A teacher in his own right, he had many high-caliber harp students, among them Paul Butterfield and Peter Wolf.

When soloing over major-key blues or rock chord changes the go-to scales are the pentatonic scale and the blues scale, a close relative of the pentatonic. You'll recall that this is done by playing cross harp, or second position, and by playing a key of harmonica that's three notes above the key the song is in, such as using an A harp to play over changes in the key of E.

When soloing over folk songs or traditional music in major keys the scale to use is the major scale, using a harmonica that's in the same key as the chord progression. Remember that all the notes of that major scale are available to you when you play using holes 4, 5, 6, and 7.

When it's time to solo over blues, rock, or folk songs that are in a minor key you'll need to use a minor scale, which is played using a harmonica that's one whole step below the key of the chord progression (for example, an F harp to play in G minor), and by playing draw harp in third position.

HARMONICA HERO: MICK JAGGER

Mick Jagger (b. 1943), as lead singer of the Rolling Stones, is one of the most prominent and visible rock stars in all of contemporary music, a position he has held for over fifty years. Although not primarily known as a harmonica player, Jagger has been a major proponent of the instrument in many ways. He has played it on almost every Rolling Stones album and at every live concert (classic tracks with Jagger on harp include "Midnight Rambler," "Can't You Hear Me Knocking," and "The Spider and the Fly"). But Jagger's larger contribution may be his bringing some of the biggest stars of blues harmonica to play on stage with the Rolling Stones, exposing them to much larger audiences. Among the harmonica greats to play with the Stones are Little Walter, Sugar Blue, and Junior Wells. Jagger also appeared as a guest artist on harmonica on the first Living Colour album, *Vivid*. Junior Wells later paid tribute to Jagger by doing a cover of the Rolling Stones song "Satisfaction."

HARMONICA HERO: JOHN LENNON

As a songwriter, singer, guitarist, and founder of the Beatles, John Lennon (1940–1980) is one of the all-time great icons of rock and roll. Lennon was also an avid harmonica player. It was the first instrument he learned to play, and his harp lines have graced numerous top Beatles songs including "Love Me Do," "Please Please Me," "Twist and Shout," "Chains," "Thank You Girl," and "I'm a Loser." John Lennon was strongly influenced by another harmonica player, Texas blues rocker Delbert McClinton. While in the UK on tour in 1962 McClinton met the young Lennon, who admired McClinton for his famous harmonica riff on Bruce Channel's number one hit "Hey! Baby." McClinton taught the riff to Lennon, who used it as inspiration for his own harmonica riff on "Love Me Do." Lennon brought the harmonica to the silver screen in the Beatles film *A Hard Day's Night* with his memorable performance on the song "I Should Have Known Better."

Playing Accompaniment/Comping

While playing accompaniment to the soloist might not seem quite as glamorous as taking the solo, the role is equally important to the final sound that is generated by the band. You'll recall that accompanying the soloist is known as "comping," which means complementing the musician taking the solo.

The role of the players who are comping is to do everything they can to make the soloist sound as good and as exciting as possible. To accomplish this you want to play notes, chords, or phrases that not only enhance what the soloist is playing, but also raise the soloist's level of excitement in order to spur him on to greater heights in his solo.

HARP TIP

A "jam track" is a special recording designed for listeners to play along with the music. It is an excellent tool for musicians who want to learn how to play ensemble. A good place for aspiring harmonica players to start is with the Mel Bay *Blues Harmonica Jam Tracks & Soloing Concepts #1*, a CD that comes with a book of lessons from harmonica whiz David Barrett. There is a second book for the more advanced.

Comping on the harmonica poses a particular set of challenges. Because the harp is usually positioned as a soloing instrument, if you start to play during somebody else's solo you tend to draw attention away from the solo—a no-no, because it's also very important in comping not to play anything that distracts attention from the soloist. But there are still ways the harmonica can comp effectively.

One way is to find a pattern to accent the rhythm while playing short staccato chords. The term *staccato* means to hold a note or chord for as short a duration as possible, like a short burst of sound. This is the opposite of notes written with a slur, which are intended to be strung together into one smooth sound; staccato notes are meant to be choppy and detached from one another. As an example, the harp might play short staccato accent chords on beats 2 and 4 of the measure, doubling the same chords that are being played in the chord progression.

Another way the harmonica can comp is to pick a note or chord and hold it for an extended time to create an organ-like background to the chord progression.

These are by no means the only ways for the harmonica to comp, so spend some time thinking of other ways you can make yourself effective, as well as listening to recordings to see how other harp players function under those circumstances.

Adding a Sectional Part or Rhythmic Accents

Another option when comping is to introduce a whole new part or feel to the music, as if you were adding a part for a horn section. One example of this is to add a short, repeating chord phrase on every fourth measure of a 12-bar blues, such as:

1	2	and	3	4	count
1-2-3 draw	1-2-3 draw	2-3-4 blow	1-2-3 draw		phrase

A sectional part like this repeating chord phrase adds excitement to the chord progression and also provides a rhythmic kick into the first measure of every line.

HARMONICA HERO: JOHN SEBASTIAN

John Benson Sebastian (b. 1944) rose to notoriety on the music scene with his band the Lovin' Spoonful in the early 1960s. The group had a long string of top hits including "Do You Believe in Magic," "Did You Ever Have to Make Up Your Mind," "Summer in the City," "Daydream," and "Nashville Cats." Sebastian took the harmonica, an instrument often associated with broken hearts, turned the frown upside down, and made it smile on top-ten pop charts all over the world. His happy blues harmonica instrumentals—such as "Night Owl Blues" from the *Do You Believe in Magic* album and "Big Noise from Speonk" from the *Daydream* album—turned a whole generation of sixties kids on to the blues harp. Sebastian also did a lot of studio work with other bands. He played on the Doors' song "Roadhouse Blues" from the *Morrison Hotel* album, on the Crosby, Stills, Nash, and Young tune "Déjà Vu" from the *Déjà Vu* album, on many tracks of *Tim Hardin 1*, and on many other influential recordings.

Rhythmic Alterations or Overlays

Still another way to go when comping is to add a rhythmic alteration or overlay to the existing rhythm. A rhythmic alteration would be something like adding a strong accent to one of the existing beats of the rhythm, such as accenting beats 2 and 4 of each measure. A rhythmic overlay would involve playing a separate new rhythm over the existing rhythm to form a polyrhythm. A *polyrhythm* is two or more rhythms being played at the same time. An example would be playing a triplet feel over straight 4/4 time, so that you were playing three beats for every beat of the 4/4 measure. Either of these approaches adds to the rhythmic interest of the music and provides the soloist with more options to play off of.

HARMONICA HERO: SONNY BOY WILLIAMSON I

John Lee Williamson (1914–1948), more commonly known as Sonny Boy Williamson I, was the first harmonica player considered to be a virtuoso on the instrument. Williamson forged the path that led to the harmonica becoming a lead instrument in blues bands everywhere. He was also a strong influence on two of the other top harmonica players ever—Little Walter and Big Walter Horton. Williamson recorded several songs that are still widely performed today. One big hit was "Good Morning, School Girl," which became a blues standard. It has been recorded and covered many times (retitled as "Good Morning Little Schoolgirl") by various groups, including Led Zeppelin, the Grateful Dead, the Yardbirds, and Ten Years After. Another of his songs, "Stop Breaking Down" (a remake of a song originally written and recorded by Robert Johnson in 1937), is a blues classic. Williamson's blazing harmonica career came to a sudden and tragic end when he was murdered in Chicago in 1948.

HARMONICA HERO: SONNY BOY WILLIAMSON II

Alex "Rice" Miller (1912–1965) did more than any other individual to bring the blues to a wider audience. He was the host of the first live radio show to focus on the blues, *King Biscuit Time*, a popular program that aired for over fifteen years. In the 1940s Miller decided to "appropriate" (read: steal) the name of nationally known blues harmonica star Sonny Boy Williamson I, aka John Lee Williamson. Because the latter never traveled to the South, this deception was allowed to continue until John Lee was murdered in Chicago in 1948. This is the reason for the number II after Miller's aka. Miller became very popular in the UK after appearing there on a folk blues tour in 1963. During that time he played and recorded with a lot of rock's royalty including Jimmy Page, Eric Burdon, and Eric Clapton.

Phrasing

In music the term *phrasing* refers to the way notes are articulated and assembled into groups. A phrase is a group of notes that expresses a musical thought or idea. If a solo is likened to a paragraph of writing, a phrase would be one sentence of that paragraph. Phrasing encompasses many factors that affect the way notes are delivered, including speeding up and slowing down, playing notes loudly or softly, accenting certain notes, the attack of each note, and more.

Another aspect of phrasing is where you choose to begin and end your phrases. If you phrase *on the bar*, you would begin your phrase on beat 1 of a measure and end it close to beat 4 of a measure. Or you could phrase *across the bar*, which means your phrase would begin somewhere in the middle of a measure and end in either in the middle or at the end of a measure.

When you play a solo you're putting together phrases, or musical ideas, that begin somewhere, progress in some direction, and wrap up at the end with a sense of conclusion.

Roots and Fifths

When you're improvising over chord changes, you can get a lot of clues about which notes to play from the chords themselves. To help you do this, it is useful to understand how chords are structured.

Every chord has a *root*, a *third*, and a *fifth*. These terms refer to the *scale degree*; that is, the notes that appear at the first, third, and fifth places on the scale form the chord. If you're looking at the key of G, the scale degrees would be:

G	A	B	C	D	E	F♯	G	A	B	C	D...	note
1	2	3	4	5	6	7	8	9	10	11	12...	scale degree

Here is the way three of the types of chords already discussed in this book are structured and what the notes are in the key of G:

Major chord	1-3-5	G-B-D
Minor chord	1-♭3-5	G-B♭-D
Seventh chord	1-3-5-♭7	G-B-D-F (the F♯ of the G major scale is flatted to an F natural)

Note that the common factor between all three chord types is that they all share the same root and fifth notes. This means that the root and the fifth are two notes that will appear and be the same exact notes in any chord with the same letter name. And that means they are both go-to notes you can play over virtually any chord. Bass players rely heavily on roots and fifths to create their bass lines for this very reason. If you're trying to figure out what the root of a chord is, you don't have to look far—it's the same as the name of the chord. The root of a C major chord is C, the root of an E7 chord is E, and so on.

HARMONICA HERO: CAREY BELL

Carey Bell (1936–2007) was a major force on the blues scene for about sixty years. He is best known for his heartfelt blues vocals and for his blazing harmonica style that grew directly out of his association with some of the greatest harp players of all time. He first played harmonica in a band with his godfather, pianist Lovie Lee, when he was just thirteen years old. Lee took Bell to Chicago in 1956, where he played with and was taught directly by harp icons Little Walter, Big Walter Horton, and Sonny Boy Williamson II. In the late 1960s he played with Earl Hooker and John Lee Hooker, and in the 1970s he played with Muddy Waters, Willie Dixon, and Hound Dog Taylor. In 1990 Bell was teamed up with harmonica luminaries Junior Wells, James Cotton, and Billy Branch to create the legendary album *Harp Attack!*

When you're going to improvise over a chord progression, before you begin take a moment to identify the roots and fifths of the chords in the progression, and then find those notes on your harmonica. This will give you a structure of notes on which you can build your solo.

You may have heard musicians talking about a 1-4-5 blues progression. The numbers 1, 4, and 5 refer to the notes of the scale you are playing in. You are playing in the key of G in the following examples of 12-bar blues, so the notes of the scale are G, A, B, C, D, E, F♯, and G. The fourth note of the scale is C and the fifth note is D, so the chords of your 1-4-5 progression will be G, C, and D. Now you'll hear a G, a C, and a D on the C harmonica.

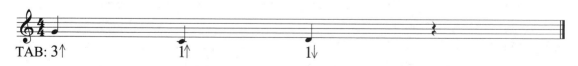

TAB: 3↑   1↑   1↓

FIGURE 6-1. ROOTS, FOURTHS, AND FIFTHS

12-Bar Blues

When musicians who have never met get together to play they might come from wildly various musical backgrounds, age groups, and cultural backgrounds, but there is one progression that transcends all these barriers and unites musicians everywhere—the 12-bar blues progression. That's because the 12-bar blues progression is so elemental that most musicians, regardless of their age, background, or level of proficiency, know it—so you need to know it too.

The 12-bar blues progression, like all chord progressions, is based on the notes of the scale of the key the progression is in. The chords, like the individual notes of the scale, are also known as *scale degrees*, and they are often indicated in music with Roman numerals. For example, if you're playing a blues in G, the scale degrees would be:

G	A	B	C	D	E	F	G	note
I	II	III	IV	V	VI	VII	VIII	scale degree

The 12-bar blues progression is the same as the 1-4-5 progression mentioned previously, with the 1, 4, and 5 referring to the scale degrees I, IV, and V.

The first degree of the scale is called the *tonic*, while the fourth degree of the scale is called the *subdominant*, and the fifth degree is called the *dominant*.

HARP TIP

The classic *wah* sound you hear often in harmonica music is created by cupping your hands tightly around the back of the harmonica and then opening the cup you've made. This effect can be used slowly to create a long *wah*, or it can be done quickly and repeatedly to create a tremolo sound.

Here's how the basic 12-bar blues progression goes:

4 bars of tonic I
2 bars of subdominant IV
2 bars of tonic I
1 bar of dominant V
1 bar of subdominant IV
2 bars of tonic I OR 1 bar of tonic I and 1 bar of dominant V

There are other variations of the 12-bar blues progression, including:

1 bar of tonic I
1 bar of subdominant IV
2 bars of tonic I
2 bars of subdominant IV
2 bars of tonic I
1 bar of dominant V
1 bar of subdominant IV
2 bars of tonic I OR 1 bar of tonic I and 1 bar of dominant V

and

4 bars of tonic I
2 bars of subdominant IV
2 bars of tonic I
2 bars dominant V
2 bars of tonic I

Such 12-bar blues progressions also come in minor keys. The chords appear in the same order and for the same duration as blues in a major key, except that in this case the chords are all minor.

Here's an example of a 12-bar blues progression. It's a slow blues feel in the key of G.

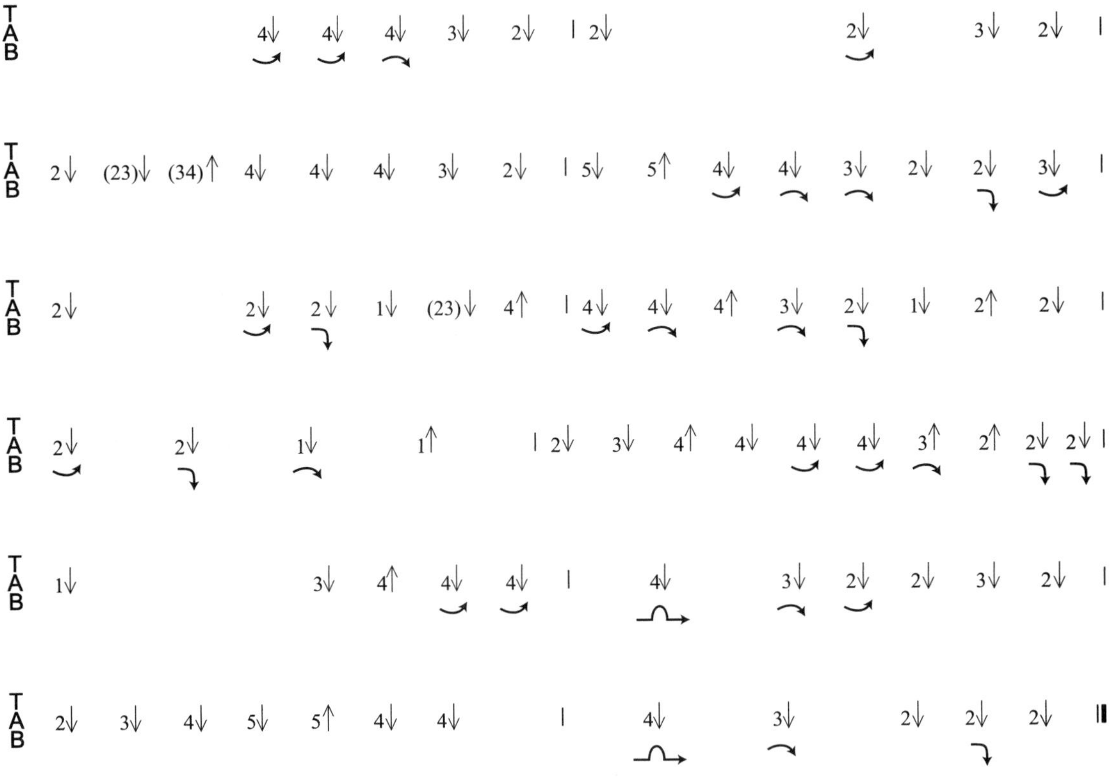

FIGURE 6-2. SLOW BLUES IN G

Here's an example of a 12-bar blues shuffle.

```
T
A    2↓(123)↓(123)↑2 ↓          3↓4↑4↓  |  4↓ 4↑ 3↓2 ↓          1↓ 2↑
B
```

```
T
A    2↓(123)↓(123)↑2↓ 1↓2↓3↓  4↑4↓  |  4↓ 4↑3↓ 2↓ 2↓(123)↓(123)↑(123)↑
B
```

```
T
A    1↓ 1↓2↓3↓4↓      4↓ 4↑  4↓  |  1↓2↓3↓4↓5↓5↑5↓4↓4↑3↓4↑4↓4↓3↓2↓
B
```

```
T
A    2↓2↓2↓2↓2↓ 2↓ 2↓2↓2↓2↓ ↓      |   2↓ 2↓ 1↓   1↓
B
```

```
T
A    (345)↑   (345)↓              ‖
B
```

FIGURE 6-3. BLUES SHUFFLE IN G

The following is an example of a 12-bar blues in the 1-4-5 progression, only with more of a jazzy feel.

FIGURE 6-4. JAZZY BLUES IN G

Tone

Usually when a musician talks about a player's tone, she is talking about the quality of the sound that is being played. Each harmonica player's tone is unique because it is partially determined by the player's physical attributes as well as being affected by external factors.

Physical attributes that are involved include the shape of the player's nasal cavity behind his face and the size of a player's hands, which can affect the sound when creating vibrato or cupping the microphone.

External factors include the type of amplifier or microphone the player uses. Trying to get what some in blues call an "authentic" tone is accomplished by manipulating the external factors. For example, buying the same vintage amplifier that Big Walter Horton was known to have played through is an example of going for an authentic tone.

HARMONICA HERO: KIM WILSON

Kim Wilson's (b. 1951) unwavering dedication to the blues was the fuel he used to spearhead a revival of blues music in the 1980s. Wilson grew up in northern California, where he was exposed to and interacted with many top bluesmen of the time, including Charlie Musselwhite and John Lee Hooker. In 1974 he moved to Austin, Texas, where he met guitarist Jimmie Vaughan, and together they founded the Fabulous Thunderbirds. During this time, Muddy Waters had occasion to play in Austin, and he was so impressed with Wilson that he became a mentor to the young harmonica player. Wilson continues to be an active artist on the blues scene.

HARMONICA HERO: BILLY BRANCH

Billy Branch (b. 1951) is known both as a faithful beacon of today's Chicago blues style and as a sort of Johnny Appleseed of the blues through his innovative music education program Blues in Schools, which has been in existence for over thirty years. Although Branch grew up in Los Angeles, he returned to Chicago in 1969, at which time he played in clubs and was tutored by harp legends Big Walter Horton, Carey Bell, and Junior Wells. Eventually he replaced Bell as the harmonica player for a six-year stint in Willie Dixon's band the Chicago Blues All Stars. Branch has also played with Muddy Waters, Albert King, and Johnny Winter, among others, and was featured on the legendary 1990 recording *Harp Attack!* with Junior Wells, James Cotton, and Carey Bell. Branch is still an active force in blues today.

The best place to begin with amplified harmonica tone is to listen to the iconic masters such as Little Walter, Big Walter Horton, and Sonny Boy Williamson II and try to match their basic sound. Qualities that are common among many harp players' tones are that they have a lot of midrange frequencies; they use a smooth, round distortion that comes from an overdriven, small-tube amplifier; and they use a moderate amount of reverb. Once you experiment and eventually develop the specific qualities in your tone that you like, you will have established your own personal harmonica tone.

That said, it is also important to be consistent with the type of music you are playing. For example, it would usually be inappropriate to have a heavily distorted amp sound on a traditional country folk tune, unless you are trying to make it an experimental piece or you are trying to make some musical point.

A harmonica player's tone comes from several places. It can come from the shape of his face, the shape of his mouth, the way he holds his throat, or the way he holds the harmonica. For instance, vibrato for a harmonica player is achieved in two different ways, either throat vibrato or hand vibrato. Hand vibrato is achieved by cupping the harmonica, then opening and closing your hand rhythmically to create the vibrato effect, similar to a trumpet player using a mute. Throat vibrato is more difficult to do because you need to control the muscles in your throat while drawing or blowing through the instrument.

Ensemble Playing

Playing music with other musicians in a duet or group setting is known as *ensemble playing*. When you're engaged in ensemble playing there are many factors you have to pay attention to in order to make sure the ensemble sounds as good as it possibly can.

The first thing you have to do is make sure that all the players are in tune with one another to avoid unwanted dissonance in the music.

HARP TIP

Dissonance and consonance are terms in music that describe the stability of tonality in the piece. *Consonance* is a sound where all the notes are in tune with each other and form a stable, pleasant sound. *Dissonance*, by contrast, is an unstable tonal quality where the combination of notes being played clash with one another and make the listener wish for resolution.

Although dissonance is a tool that's sometimes purposely used by composers to make the listener uncomfortable for artistic purposes, it's certainly not something you want to have in your sound just because the group is out of tune.

Ensemble playing requires a different kind of listening than solo playing in that you have to divide your attention between what you are playing and what all the other musicians are playing. There's a constant give and take occurring between all the musicians that requires attentive listening so that you can use that information to guide what you are playing.

Some of the factors you'll need to pay attention to in ensemble playing are:

- **Balance:** This is the relationship between the volumes of the different instruments. No musician should be overly loud, even when soloing, to the point where he is making it hard to hear the other musicians. At the same time, no musician should be so soft that the part he is playing becomes irrelevant or inaudible.
- **Style:** Follow the accepted practices of the genre of music you're playing. For example, you wouldn't want to try to play a folk song over a blues-style song. Different genres of music also have different general approaches used by the soloists in improvising their solos.

HARMONICA HERO: MARK HUMMEL

Mark Hummel (b. 1955) is widely known for his harmonica style that blends the rich tradition of harmonica greats such as Little Walter and Sonny Boy Williamson II with a swing feel and jazz phrasing, a fusion of influences that is known as West Coast blues. He is considered to be one of the top harmonica players on the contemporary blues scene. Hummel has performed with area musicians including Sonny Lane and Mississippi Johnny Waters. In 1980 he formed the Blues Survivors, a group that continues to record and perform today.

HARMONICA HERO: ROD PIAZZA

Rod Piazza (b. 1947) is recognized for his searing harmonica tone and technical virtuosity that blends jazz phrasing with blues technique. He is also considered one of today's top blues songwriters. Piazza began his professional career at the age of eighteen in Los Angeles with his own band, as well as performing with blues greats Big Mama Thornton, T-Bone Walker, and Big Joe Turner. In 1968 he teamed up with the legendary George "Harmonica" Smith to form the group Bacon Fat, which performed and recorded for fifteen years. In 1980 Piazza formed the Mighty Flyers with keyboard player Honey Alexander (now Piazza's wife), a protégé of Otis Spann. The band, which is considered to be pushing the boundaries of modern blues music, continues to perform today.

- **Chord progression:** Make sure the notes you're choosing are appropriate for the key and the type of scale being used. For example, if the band is playing a blues progression, it wouldn't work to try to play a solo using a major scale. You'll also need to know where the solos begin and end, meaning the length of one *chorus*, defined as one time through the progression.
- **Dynamics:** This is how loudly or softly the group as a whole is playing. It's especially important to be sensitive to where the music is going dynamically and make sure you're in fluid sync with the other musicians, because the dynamics of music play a large part in conveying the overall mood. If the dynamics are building to a peak, you want to be raising the roof in your part too. If they're ramping down, you should lower your own volume and relax your feel as well so that the group as a whole can make smooth dynamic changes.
- **Signals:** This is how musicians communicate with each other in the moment so that they can agree about where to take the music next. These signals might be quick spoken words, hand gestures, or even just the meaningful meeting of eyes.

HARMONICA HERO: JIMMY REED

Jimmy Reed was one of the most popular stars in blues in the 1950s and 1960s, and is widely considered to have been the artist that first drew large white audiences to blues music. He is best known for creating a large body of blues songs that, because of their relatively simple structures, became some of the most heavily covered songs in all of blues. These songs include "Big Boss Man," "Baby What You Want Me to Do," and "Ain't That Lovin' You, Baby." Reed played with longtime friend, guitarist Eddie Taylor. Together the two created eighteen top-twenty hits on the R & B charts in the late 1950s and early 1960s. Unfortunately, Reed suffered from both crippling alcoholism and undiagnosed epilepsy, a combination that brought his meteoric career to an early close with his death in 1976.

This might seem like a lot of things to pay attention to at one time, but as you get more experience playing with others you'll find that your focus will expand to take in all these factors automatically and adjust for them as you go along.

Band Etiquette

If you want to play ensemble with other musicians, it will help if you get an A for "plays well with others" on your report card. Ensemble playing demands that you pay attention to your fellow musicians and what they're doing and playing at all times, especially if you hope to be invited back a second time.

There are times when it's best *not* to play when playing ensemble, which is important when discussing bandstand etiquette. Don't play under the following circumstances:

- When the singer is singing, except during breaks in the vocals.
- When someone else is taking a solo, except for possibly comping for them.
- If you haven't figured out the sound of the chord progression yet, or if you get confused about where you are in the progression during a song. Then jump in when you get your bearings.

If you pay careful attention to your band etiquette, you'll be making a big contribution to the overall sound of your ensemble, as well as making yourself a popular player among other musicians.

Playing Along with Recordings

One excellent way to practice your improvisation and your ensemble playing at the same time is to play along with recordings. But before you begin to do that you'll need to know what key the song you're listening to is in so that you can select the right harmonica to use. Here are a couple of tricks you can use to do that.

First, listen carefully to the opening chord of the song—way more often than not, that first chord will be the root chord of the key the song is in.

Second, pull out your C harmonica and check the sound of the opening chord against every note in the C major scale (holes 4, 5, 6, and 7) to see which one matches the key. If the chord doesn't exactly match one of those notes the song is probably in a flatted or sharped key, which will be a half step above or below one of the harmonica notes.

Chapter 7

PRACTICING

The desire and drive to play the harmonica well will fuel your way to becoming a good player, but practice is the road you take to get there. If your practicing is intermittent, random, and undirected, that road will be winding with lots of forks and dead ends. But if you make your practice habits focused and effective, that road can be an expressway to becoming a great player.

Why Practice?

If anyone ever forced you to take music lessons as a child when you had no such motivation of your own, the words "go practice" can evoke terrible memories of mind-numbing boredom. Even skilled musicians who have practiced hard for years have days when practicing is the last thing they feel like doing.

You're lucky to have the one thing necessary to make sure practicing won't be a bore—the desire to play the harmonica! When you're practicing something you really want to get good at, time flies by. You might wonder how musicians could sit down and practice for hours at a time. The reason is it can seem like minutes to them because they're so absorbed in what they're doing, and they're having fun.

The hardest thing about practicing is sitting down and beginning. Before you physically sit down in your practice chair, anything and everything will distract you, but once you start practicing, all the fun of playing the harmonica will keep you entertained.

Furthermore, as you progress, your own improvement will become a huge motivator for you to keep practicing. Ultimately the goal is to push your skills to the limit of what is possible on your instrument—and then beyond!

Practice at Regular Times

Because simply beginning is one of the biggest barriers to practicing, it helps to have a regular time designated as your practice time. Factors you might consider when trying to figure out your optimal practice time include:

- The times of day when you have the most energy.
- The times when the fewest people are around who might be disturbed by your practicing, including family, roommates, and neighbors.
- The times when you're least likely to be distracted by other people, your smartphone, and so on.

Having a regular practice time has many benefits. For one thing, it carves time out of your daily schedule to prevent conflicts with other activities. It also ensures that you will have the expectation of practicing every day. Try your best to practice regularly at your practice time, not skipping days but just practicing less on your off days. Aiming to practice for one hour a day is a good place to begin if you want to show rapid improvement, but even fifteen or twenty minutes a day is an acceptable place to start. You might even find yourself joining the five-hours-a-day crowd someday soon!

Get Organized and Be Prepared

Whatever amount of time you spend practicing, you want to make the most of it. For that reason it's important to organize your practice time and to create your own personalized practice routine.

One important part of organizing your routine is to make sure you allow time every day to get some practice in critical areas. This means you should work in segments where you practice scales, chords, tongue blocking and slapping, and whole songs you want to learn. As your technique develops you can add working on your tone, your vibrato, breath control, and other more advanced techniques. Make a plan for your practice sessions with a list of the things you want to work on, and plan your practice time so that at least a few minutes are devoted to each of these areas.

HARP TIP

A metronome is a device that makes a click or other sound at regular intervals. Musicians use the device to practice by setting a certain number of beats per minute.

Another important part of getting organized is setting up a practice area for yourself somewhere in your house, or elsewhere, that's equipped with the following items:

- A *comfortable chair* with a back that allows you to sit up straight
- A *music stand* so that you can put your practice notebook in a place where it's right in front of your eyes without having to hold it
- A *metronome* for practicing scales and playing in time in general
- A *notebook* to keep your lists of practice routines, exercises, and other inspirations
- A *recording device* to record your progress for self-evaluation such as your smartphone or a digital recorder
- A *backup harmonica* for those days when your own harp blows a reed or stops working for any other reason

Make a point of adding new techniques and exercises to practice to your list often, and go back frequently to refresh yourself on earlier material.

Relax and Focus

When you're getting ready to practice, it's good to take a few moments to relax your body and focus your mind. Chances are your shoulders, neck, and jaw are still carrying the tensions of the day, and those areas are precisely the areas you need to be relaxed to play well. Your mind is also likely to be full of the details of your day and will need a focusing exercise or two to remove those distractions. You'll want to be as relaxed and focused as possible to make the most of your practice time.

To unwind your body, close your eyes and consciously tell each area of your upper body to relax, like a check list: relax your scalp, relax your eyes, relax your neck, relax your shoulders…and as you do, focus on relaxing those individual muscle areas. This technique is very effective.

HARMONICA HERO: FRÉDÉRIC YONNET

"Fred" Yonnet (b. 1973) is an urban jazz harmonicist. He was born in France and has been playing the harmonica since he was a child. He now plays gigs around the United States and conducts workshops and master classes for aspiring harmonica players. He has played with an impressive list of musicians, including Stevie Wonder and Prince, songwriter David Foster, Ed Sheeran, the Jonas Brothers, John Legend, Erykah Badu, John Mayer, and India Arie Simpson (best known as India.Arie).

To focus your mind, you might start with the exercise of breathing through the harp that was discussed earlier—first breathe out slowly through holes 1-2-3, and then inhale slowly through the same three holes, listening as your breath is translated into sound on your instrument.

One more good exercise for focusing your mind on practicing is to think about *why* you're practicing—whether it's to sound as good as someone you've heard on harmonica, or to become a performer, or just to be able to blow people away who didn't know you'd been studying harmonica. Envision your goal while you practice. Hold it out in front of you like a carrot on a stick.

Finally, start your actual practice session by warming up with easy things that you can already play to loosen up your muscles and get into the swing of practicing.

Listening Is Practicing Too

One of the most important parts of developing as a musician is listening to a lot of music. It's especially critical to listen to other harmonica players, but any music you listen to has valuable lessons to teach you.

When listening to other harmonica players, check out their tone on the instrument (which is a function of their playing and their amplification if they're playing through a microphone—more on this later), the way they phrase their musical ideas, and the way they interact with their band. When you hear sounds you like, try to emulate them. When you hear sounds you don't like, avoid them in your own playing.

In particular, listen for riffs you can "steal" and use them in your own playing. "Steal" is in quotes because the borrowing of riffs is a long-standing and honorable tradition in music. The famous jazz guitarist Barney Kessel once said, "Borrow from one guy—that's plagiarism. Borrow from two or more—that's research." In fact, all musicians are the sum of their musical influences, and what makes each musician unique is that everybody's combination of influences is different.

When you find a riff you like and want to learn, listen to it over and over again until you know how it goes. Then slow the tempo way down and learn the riff at a tempo at which you can play it, speeding it up gradually once you know it.

Playing along with recordings is another excellent form of practice. It gives you the opportunity to play along with a band—often a great band—that affords you a very different and more lively experience than practicing alone with a metronome. There are even recordings that purposely leave out the harmonica part so you can play it yourself. The best-known manufacturer of such recordings is Music Minus One, but there are others as well.

Note here that the music you listen to will be in a variety of keys, so you'll require a variety of harmonicas in keys other than C to play along. A good set of other harmonicas to start with would be an A harp, a D harp, an E harp, and an F harp, which will allow you to play cross harp for most common blues songs in the keys of E, A, B, and C, besides the key of G that you can play on your C harmonica.

If you already know what kind of music you want to play, listen to and practice in that style as much as possible after learning the fundamentals of playing harmonica.

HARP TIP

If you're listening to a recording and you absolutely can't figure out what the key of the song is, remember that the key could be flatted or sharped, meaning that it's a half step off from the keys of any of your harmonicas. This is the case, for example, with many Little Walter recordings that are in the key of E♭ and require an A♭ harmonica to play cross harp.

Another tremendously valuable form of listening is listening to yourself play. This allows you to get outside your own head and body and hear what you sound like from the outside, from a listener's point of view. It's a great idea to have your smartphone sitting next to you when you practice so you can record yourself and listen back later to evaluate yourself.

Break It Down

The human brain can only absorb so much new information at one time, so if you're trying to learn a big block of new material you'll need to break it down into manageable segments.

If you're having a hard time learning a line or phrase, split it in half or divide it into smaller phrases that you can deal with effectively. Try to isolate the hardest parts or the ones you're having the most trouble with and practice them until they're as strong as any other part.

In fact, this is a good concept for your overall playing as well—if you're looking for large leaps forward in your technique, try making the weakest aspect of your playing the strongest one instead through focusing on that aspect above others until you are proficient.

Be musical in your practicing. Don't think of exercises as just a series of notes you have to make your way through. Instead, treat exercises like they're real music that you have to play with expression and emotional content—that's the way you want your playing to be, so it's what you should always be practicing.

Slow Down

One of the biggest mistakes musicians make at the beginning is to try to learn new music at too fast a tempo. Inevitably this leads to making a lot of mistakes, and by making the same mistakes over and over again you're effectively teaching your brain how to play wrong.

That's because as you learn new things you're building neural pathways, which means you're actually building new parts of your brain! Once you've practiced mistakes often enough they become ingrained in your mind by these new neural pathways, and they are much more difficult to correct later.

HARP TIP

There are software programs now that do what used to be impossible—they slow down the speed of music without changing the pitch, giving you the ideal situation for learning new, and especially difficult, pieces of music. One good example is the Amazing Slow Downer. Find it at RoniMusic.com.

This is where your metronome comes in. It's best to learn any new scale, rhythm, or song at a very slow tempo to begin with so that you can fully analyze it and play the notes cleanly with your current skill level. Playing along with the metronome ensures that you will be playing in solid, even time at whatever speed you practice. Once you can play the new material perfectly at the slow tempo, speed up the metronome a little and practice until you can play the material perfectly at the new tempo. Then speed up the metronome again. This process ensures that your technique will develop without built-in flaws. Your technique is built from the ground up, and a weak foundation will come back to haunt you later when you can't build advanced techniques on top of it.

If you're playing a piece of music and you hit a rough spot that you can't play through without mistakes, stop and cut the tempo in half on your metronome. This may feel exaggeratedly slow at the time, but it makes it easy for you to play the notes correctly, and as you play them correctly you're building those good new neural pathways. Focus on the exact place where your mistakes are occurring, rather than going all the way back to the beginning of the piece just to work on your trouble spot. Once you can play the notes correctly, you can insert your clean, new phrase back into the piece at the original tempo.

Eventually these fundamental techniques become rote and you can stop focusing on them—they'll automatically become part of your technique and your muscle memory.

HARP TIP

Muscle memory is a phenomenon where your brain and the muscle groups you need to play your instrument (including your hands, fingers, mouth, tongue, and throat) form a bond that can function while bypassing your conscious mind. Expert players have spoken of times when in performance they forgot an upcoming passage and, while their brain panicked, their body played right through the section correctly!

HARP TIP

When you're done playing your harmonica, always rap the instrument (with the holes pointing down) several times against your leg or the palm of your hand to eliminate excess saliva and anything else that might have gotten inside. Be sure your harp is completely dry before you put it away.

While your goal is to build up speed in your playing, it's not enough just to be able to play fast—you have to be in control of your technique at whatever speed you're playing to be a great player. Make sure that you're not practicing phrases faster than you can play them cleanly and correctly—perfect beats fast every time.

Evaluate Yourself Honestly, but Stay Positive and Have Fun!

Studying music and practicing hard does not come without periods of frustration. You will have weeks where you're quite impressed with yourself for the obvious progress you're making. Then there will be those times—even long periods—where you feel like you're making absolutely no progress at all. That's because you've reached a plateau.

The fact is, you won't see obvious improvement every single day that you practice, and there will be long stretches when you wonder what the bleep your efforts are producing, since nothing seems to be changing about your playing. Be assured that there is light at the end of this tunnel. You'll wake up one morning and be able to play a riff that's been eluding you, just like magic. It's the interest on your deposit.

Your brain will always be ahead of your technique. This is true even for the greatest musicians. The unattainable goal is to be able to play anything your brain can conceive with perfect technical execution. And the fact that this is unattainable is a good thing—it means you'll always have something to strive for!

That's the challenge that drives you forward and ensures that practicing will never be a waste of your time.

Chapter 8

GEAR AND ACCESSORIES

If you're planning to play with other musicians in a band or other group setting, you're going to need amplification to be heard. But amplification isn't just about getting louder—different microphones and amplifiers have a major effect on your tone, which is the voice through which all your playing is expressed. This chapter explores the microphones, amplifiers, and effects you'll need to get started.

Microphones

A microphone has one job and that is to collect sound and convert it to electricity. While all microphones perform this function, they each have their own unique sound qualities that affect your tone. The following are some of the commonly available microphones you might choose.

AKG C414

The AKG C414 is an extremely sensitive condenser microphone that gives a clean, faithful sound with no distortion. If you're looking for an exact reproduction of your source sound, this type of clean studio mic is for you. The AKG C414 is currently available for about $1,000.

HARP TIP

Perhaps the most important considerations about purchasing harmonica-related gear and accessories are to think about what style of music you're playing, where you're playing, and your budget. (More expensive equipment isn't always better.) If you can, try out equipment before you purchase it, and be sure it fits your style of play and most common venue (even if that's your own living room).

Shure SM58

The Shure SM58 is one of the workhorses of the microphone world. This is the mic you're most likely to run across on stage at concerts or clubs because of its reliability and durability. Translation—these mics are hard to kill, no matter what happens to them. The SM58 has a warm sound and will produce some distortion if the signal is loud going into the mic, which can be good for your tone. It is currently available for $100. The Shure SM58 ball microphone is the one you're most likely to come across in most clubs.

Shure 520DX

The Shure 520DX Green Bullet is the current model of the legendary Shure 520, originally manufactured by Shure from 1949 to 1977. After being discontinued for several years, the mic was reintroduced as the Shure 520D, made in Mexico.

Many of the Chicago sound players used this type of mic, and ever since Little Walter, Big Walter Horton, and Sonny Boy Williamson came on the scene, the standard for blues harp players has been the Green Bullet microphone, a high-impedance crystal mic. Originally these were army-issue microphones, which might explain why there were so many of them around. Later they were called into action as taxi dispatching mics because their intense reproduction of the midrange made them easy to hear over traffic noise.

The current version of the Shure Green Bullet mic is the 520DX model, which has many of the advantages and fewer of the foibles of the earlier microphones. The 520DX is less likely to feedback and, because the crystal has been replaced by solid state electronics, it is less fragile. The size and shape are also perfect for cupping the mic with the harmonica. The 520DX has a built in ¼-inch guitar-style plug on a good length of cable. It is suitable for most amplifiers, and the new volume knob provides much better control of the mic while playing. It is currently available for $120.

HARP TIP

Keeping multiple harmonicas organized can be tricky. Some players use a leather belt or bandoleer with pockets for each harp, keeping them in order by key and remembering the order for quick access. Or you can put stickers on them, which are easy to read and can be seen in situations with little light.

There is a big difference between other microphones and the way a Green Bullet translates sound into electricity. When you play through it you may find that your whole presence becomes more focused on your playing, because this microphone is made for this instrument alone. You can, and some people do, sing through a Green Bullet mic, but its true purpose is for playing electric blues harmonica. Many other harmonica microphones are out there, but none have the tried-and-true reputation of the Green Bullet.

The biggest disadvantage of the Green Bullet mics is that they are some-what heavy when compared to other Shure stage mics.

Another popular harmonica microphone is the Beyerdynamic M160 Double Ribbon, which comes close to more expensive condenser microphones in its clean, flat response ($700).

Amplifiers

Equally important to your choice of microphone is the amplifier you select to plug it into. Amplifiers come in all shapes and sizes, and the amp that's right for you will depend on the purpose you're using it for. That said, there are certain qualities in an amp that are considered desirable for harmonica players.

The first is that tube amplifiers are generally considered to be better than solid-state amplifiers because they have a warmer, rounder sound. The second is that smaller amplifiers are generally considered to be a better choice than large amps, both because they are portable and easy to carry and because their volume controls can be turned up much louder, which creates the smooth, distorted sustain that many players are looking for. Note that small amps might have to be amplified themselves with a microphone through a PA system to bring you up to the volume level of the other instruments you're playing with.

Peavey Mark IV

A solid-state vintage Peavey Mark IV bass head with two 15-inch speakers is one example of the clean, big-amp approach, which has two primary advantages—it provides a very clean sound and it provides a very loud sound. Bass amps have the advantage of not boosting the high and midrange frequencies that cause feedback, as well as emphasizing the desirable bass range of the instrument. This particular rig is quite large—the speaker cabinet takes two people to carry—but it's perfect for projecting loud, undistorted harmonica sound. Cost varies across stores and auction websites.

HARP TIP

Older, heavier tube amps often get the best sound, but those are usually going to be found in pawn shops. MESA/Boogie still makes good tube-based amps. Look for them at www.mesaboogie.com.

Fender Super Reverb

A Fender Super Reverb tube amp is an example of the midsized amplifier approach. This is an all-tube 45-watt amplifier in a combo cabinet with four 10-inch speakers and built-in reverb and tremolo. This amp weighs 65 pounds, so it's moderately portable. It provides a loud, warm sound, and because it is equipped with a master volume control, it's easy to create a beautiful over-driven sustain that can be either loud or soft. Fender no longer makes them, but you can sometimes find used ones for around $1,500.

Fender Blues Junior

A Fender Blues Junior tube amp is one of the most sought-after amplifiers among harmonica players, and is an example of the small amplifier approach. This is an all-tube 15-watt amplifier in a combo cabinet with one 12-inch speaker and built-in reverb. This amp only weighs 31 pounds, so it's extremely portable. Because the amp is small it can be turned up to a loud volume to create overdriven sustain without being too loud compared to other instruments. The Blues Junior amp also has a "fat switch" that fattens up the bottom end of the sound and makes the overall sound rounder by boosting the input signal. It is currently available for $600.

Other popular harmonica amplifiers include the Fender '59 Bassman reissue bass amp, which combines the advantages of a bass amp with the advantages of an all-tube amp for another midsized option, and the small Fender Pro Junior (a smaller version of the Blues Junior) and Fender Champ amps. Note that none of these amplifiers have built-in reverb.

Here are a couple of general tips about using an amplifier when playing harmonica. First, if you're using a guitar amplifier as opposed to a bass amp, you'll have to turn the treble and middle knobs down pretty low to avoid feedback.

HARMONICA HERO: HOWARD LEVY

Howard Levy (b. 1951) is one of the most outstanding harmonica players of his generation. In addition to his absolute mastery of the instrument, Levy is credited with the development of new techniques that dramatically expanded the musical possibilities of the diatonic harmonica, the most important of which is the overblow, which allowed the harmonica to produce notes never before available on the instrument. In addition, he is unrivalled for the number of different musical styles in which he can play fluently, which include jazz, classical, rock, folk, Latin, and world music. Levy's professional music career began in Chicago, where he played with Tom Paxton, Steve Goodman, and John Prine, among others. In 1988 he played with Béla Fleck and the Flecktones at a folk festival in Canada, and in 1989 he joined the group, recording and touring with them for four years, a stint that made him widely known as a harmonica genius. Levy has also played and recorded with a myriad of top artists including Dolly Parton, Jerry Garcia, Paul Simon, Jack Bruce, Laurie Anderson, Paquito D'Rivera, Kenny Loggins, and Art Lande. Levy continues to be a major force in the world of harmonica.

HARP TIP

Feedback is usually responsible for the sudden accidental high-pitched shrieking you've heard at events where microphones are being used. It's a result of a loop being formed where the microphone is taking in sound, amplifying it, and sending it out through speakers, and the resulting louder sound is then taken back in by the microphone. As this process is repeated the loud shriek builds in the speakers.

Second, the further you place your amplifier away from where you are standing with the microphone, the less chance of feedback you'll have. That's because feedback is created when the microphone is pointing at the speakers of the amp. Another good trick for avoiding feedback is to place your amplifier in front of you with the speaker facing away from you.

Effects Boxes

Once you've established your microphone and your amplifier sounds, you might want to add effects boxes to your rig to further alter your overall sound. For harmonica, the first two most sought-after effects that add to your sound are reverb and echo.

Reverb is short for reverberation, which is the bouncing of sound waves off of many different surfaces in an enclosed space at one time. If you've ever been in a large empty room and shouted or clapped your hands, you've heard all the "extra" sound that's left bouncing around the room after your original sound has ended—that's reverberation. Each of the many individual reflected sounds reaches your ears at a different time, which is why the reverberation continues after the original sound is gone.

HARMONICA HERO: WILLIAM CLARKE

William Clarke (1951–1996) was best known for his original voice on blues harmonica, which combined elements of the Chicago blues sound with West Coast blues, and for his virtuosity on the chromatic harmonica. Clarke studied both diatonic and chromatic harmonica directly with George "Harmonica" Smith, with whom he performed and recorded for six years. He went on to record a string of solo albums that sold well and enabled him to tour continuously and cemented his reputation as a master of the harmonica as well as an excellent singer and songwriter. Clarke's innovations on the harmonica live on.

Because reverb is often built in to amplifiers, it is not being looked at as a separate effect in this chapter, but be advised that reverb is also available as a separate effect if you end up with an amp that doesn't come with it.

Echo is the repeated reproduction of the original sound. If you've ever shouted across a canyon and heard your words repeated a couple of seconds later, you know what an echo sounds like.

Echo effects are created electronically using an analog or, more commonly, a *digital delay*. Adding delay adds excitement and three-dimensionality to your overall sound. What the digital delay is doing is making a copy of your original sound and then repeating it after a short delay, hence the name.

Echo can be added in a couple of different basic ways. Having just one echo that is placed very tightly against the original sound creates a *doubling* effect, as if two harmonicas were playing exactly the same thing. Having just one echo with a little more separation from the original sound creates a *slapback* sound, which is like the sound of an instrument bouncing once off the back wall of a room, giving your notes a concert-hall quality. The more space between the original sound and the echo, the bigger the "room" sounds. Having more than one echo repeat after your original sound is called *regeneration* because the output from the delay is being fed back into the input over and over again. This creates the sound of multiple echoes that fade in volume as they repeat.

Note that the "feedback" knob is the one on digital delays that controls the number of repeats of the echo.

One note of caution with digital delays—you have to be careful that the timing of the repeats does not interfere with the rhythm of the song you're playing. Repeats of your sound that are not in time with the rhythm will throw the whole band off.

Another useful effect for harmonica players is *distortion*. You'll recall that turning small amps up loud produces a desirable distortion that is characterized by a smooth hornlike sustain. The amp is producing this sound because it is being overdriven by the high-volume setting. This type of distortion is created electronically by using an effect called an *overdrive* that produces the same effect by overdriving its own internal amplifier. If you're playing through a large amp that you can't turn up loud enough to produce natural distortion, an overdrive is the solution to getting the sustain you want at lower volumes.

Note that although using effects to create this sound works well, a good tube amp that has a nice distorted sound and a good microphone will create that classic Chicago sound better than any configuration of effects boxes.

HARP TIP

The Trumpet Call harmonica made by Hohner in 1906 looked impressive, but that's where the allure ended—the five dramatic brass bells protruding from the back of the harmonica were purely decorative and had no effect on the instrument's sound.

One more effect that sounds good with harmonica is tremolo. *Tremolo* is created by running the volume control of the amplifier through a slow wave form that uniformly raises and lowers the volume at an even pace. This subtle wavering of the volume overlays the sound with a pleasant texture. Many amplifiers, including the Fender Super Reverb discussed previously, come with built-in tremolo.

There are boxes that will make tremolo sound, but nothing in a tremolo sounds as good as an old amplifier. In general, smaller tube amplifiers are preferable. They overdrive easily and they minimize the problems with feedback.

Customizing

Even after you've found your microphone, amplifier, and effects, you still might be searching for a further refinement of your sound. Another avenue you can explore for this purpose is to alter one or more of the pieces of equipment you're currently using.

HARMONICA HERO: ADAM GUSSOW

Adam Gussow (b. 1958) is recognized for his roots approach to the harmonica, but also for incorporating elements of rock, jazz, and fusion into his eclectic harp style. Gussow was born in Rockland County, New York, in 1958. He started playing harmonica in high school, influenced by artists such as Little Walter and James Cotton. In 1985 he met guitarist and blues legend Sterling Magee, who was playing on the street in Harlem, and who went on to become his longtime music partner. After a long stint together as popular street musicians in Harlem, the pair toured and recorded together for eight years. Gussow was also notably featured in the U2 film *Rattle and Hum* in 1988. Gussow continues to play, teach, and write in Oxford, Mississippi.

As far as your harmonica is concerned, options include retuning your reed plates or even replacing them with plates of an entirely different scale. Hohner makes a series of harmonicas known as 532/20 Blues Harp (MS), with combs, reed plates, and covers that can be easily interchanged (the MS stands for "modular system"), allowing you to easily customize your harp. Lee Oskar harmonicas are also designed to have parts replaced or interchanged.

Regarding your amplifier, the easiest modification and the one most likely to make a big difference in your sound is to replace the speaker. The speaker is the voice of your amp, and different brands and models of speakers have varying sound qualities. Some speaker manufacturers, such as Jensen, offer a "tone chart" that describes the differences in sound between their various speakers.

It's even possible to customize some microphones. The popular Green Bullet mics use microphone elements to pick up the sound. Different microphone elements have different sound qualities, and they can be interchanged inside the Shure 520 Bullet shell.

Cables and Adapters

Once you get your equipment to the location where you'll be playing, the next step is to get it all to work well in a foreign environment (read: not your living room). Here's a list of items you'll need to ensure that you're able to play when the moment comes:

- A *microphone cable* to connect your mic to your amplifier or effects. If you're going to be standing far away from your amp you might also need a *microphone extension cable.*
- A heavy-duty *extension cord* for your amp. Most amp power cords are only about 6 feet long, and the nearest plug might be further away. Also recommended—a couple of three-prong or two-prong *plug adapters* and an *extra plug with screw terminals* for your power cord for that wonderful moment when your plug gets severed right before you're supposed to begin playing.

- An *extra fuse* for your amplifier. Fuses don't blow that often, but when they do it's a show-stopper.
- If you play through a high-impedance microphone and you want to plug into a low-impedance PA system, you might need a *direct box* that accepts your mic's ¼-inch plug and comes out with a three-pin balanced output jack.

Minor-Key Tunings

Harmonicas come in other tunings besides the diatonic Richter tuning and chromatic tuning. Some of the most interesting tunings are the minor-key tunings. Lee Oskar offers harmonicas in two minor tunings, the natural minor and the harmonic minor scales. The natural minor is used to play straight minor-key songs, while the harmonic minor has an Eastern European or "ethnic" sound to it.

These minor-key harps are interesting because they blast you into a whole new tonal universe and break your head temporarily out of the diatonic tuning.

HARMONICA HERO: MICKEY RAPHAEL

Mickey Raphael (b. 1951) is best known for his role as harmonica player for Willie Nelson, a position he has held for over thirty years. Rafael was born in Dallas in 1952. In 1973 he was invited to an informal jam session with Willie Nelson and Charlie Pride, among others. Nelson was so impressed with Raphael that he invited him to play a prestigious gig at New York City's Max's Kansas City, and the rest, as they say, is history. In addition to his longtime association with Nelson, Raphael has been a prolific studio musician, recording with U2, Neil Young, Elton John, Vince Gill, and Emmy Lou Harris, among others. He is still an active musician playing in Nelson's band.

Appendix A

THE ESSENTIAL HARMONICA RECORDINGS

Early Blues

Big Mama Thornton, *The Complete Vanguard Recordings*

Big Walter Horton, *They Call Me Big Walter*

Carey Bell, *Heartaches and Pain*

George "Harmonica" Smith, *Harmonica Ace: The Modern Masters*

James Cotton, *Pure Cotton*

Jimmy Reed, *Blues Masters: The Very Best of Jimmy Reed*

Junior Wells, *Hoodoo Man Blues*

Little Walter, *His Best: The Chess 50th Anniversary Collection*

Paul Oscher, *Alone with the Blues*

Sonny Boy Williamson I, *The Bluebird Recordings: 1937–1938*

Sonny Boy Williamson II, *His Best: The Chess 50th Anniversary Collection*

Sonny Terry and Brownie McGhee, *Brownie McGhee and Sonny Terry Sing*

Modern Blues

Billy Branch, Carey Bell, James Cotton, and Junior Wells, *Harp Attack!*

Butterfield Blues Band, *East-West*

Charlie Musselwhite, *Delta Hardware*

John Mayall, *Blues Breakers with Eric Clapton*

Little Charlie and the Nightcats, *Nine Lives*

Norton Buffalo and the Knockouts, *King of the Highway*

Paul Butterfield, "Mystery Train" and "Mannish Boy," featured in *The Band: The Last Waltz*

Satan and Adam (Sterling Magee and Adam Gussow), *Harlem Blues*

Sugar Blue, *Blues Explosion*

Various Artists, *What's Shakin'*

Classic Rock

Black Sabbath, "The Wizard" (single)

Bruce Springsteen, *Nebraska*

Canned Heat, "On the Road Again" (single)

J. Geils Band, *"Live" Full House*

Led Zeppelin, "When the Levee Breaks" (single)

Folk and Country

Bob Dylan, *Blonde on Blonde*

John Sebastian, *Do You Believe in Magic*

Jazz

Béla Fleck and the Flecktones, *Flight of the Cosmic Hippo*

Howard Levy, *The Molinaro-Levy Project: Live*

Toots Thielemans, *Only Trust Your Heart*

The 1980s and 1990s

Blues Traveler, *Four*

Eurythmics, "Missionary Man" (single)

Neil Young, *Harvest Moon*

Pretenders, "Middle of the Road" (single)

The 2000s

Adam Gussow, *Kick and Stomp*

Charlie Musselwhite, *The Well*

Frédéric Yonnet, *Blowing Your Mind in Every Key of the Harp*

Howard Levy, *Concerto for Diatonic Harmonica and Orchestra*

Sugar Blue, *Raw Sugar (Live)*

Appendix B

RESOURCES

Books

Jon Gindick and Barry Geller, *Country and Blues Harmonica for the Musically Hopeless* (Klutz Press)

Paul Butterfield, *Paul Butterfield—Blues Harmonica Master Class: Book/CD Pack* (Homespun-Pap/Com)

DVDs and Online Tutorials

Adam Gussow, "Learn Blues Harmonica 101," https://youtu.be/79vSshFzT3w

John Popper, "How to Get Started: Harmonica Lessons," https://youtu .be/B_PhHrBEeNI

John Sebastian, *John Sebastian Teaches Blues Harmonica*, DVD (Homespun)

Jazz and Blues Experience. "Little Walter: The Blues Harmonica Legend," https://youtu.be/uHG7ezpPB54

Norton Buffalo, *Harmonica Power! Norton Buffalo's Blues Techniques*, DVD or software (Homespun)

Peter Madcat Ruth, *Anyone Can Play Harmonica: An Easy Guide to Getting Started*, DVD (Homespun)

Websites

www.hohnerusa.com: The Hohner website—click on "Instruments" and "Harmonicas" to get to the good stuff

www.hunterharp.com/harplink.htm: A good portal to harmonica websites of all kinds, including artist sites

www.modernbluesharmonica.com: Instructional videos, blues harp tabs, and recordings by Adam Gussow

www.patmissin.com: Pat Missin, harmonica player, teacher, technician, and historian, is a wealth of information about everything harmonica

www.spah.org: Website of the Society for the Preservation and Advancement of the Harmonica

www.youtube.com/user/fredyonnet: Frédéric Yonnet's work

Appendix C

GLOSSARY

accent
To play a beat or note more loudly than the beats or notes surrounding it, thereby emphasizing it.

arpeggio
A chord that is played one note at a time in sequential order, either ascending or descending.

articulation syllables
Letter sounds like "D" and "T" that you make with your mouth at the beginning of each note to release a concentrated amount of air that produces the hard attack.

attack
The way a note begins, from softly to loudly and from smoothly to sharply.

balance
The relationship between the volumes of the different instruments playing together.

bar lines
The vertical lines that divide measures, also known as "bars," in musical notation.

bass clef
Signified by this symbol 𝄢. The lines of the staff, from bottom to top, represent G B D F A.

beat
The pulse of a piece of music, usually the note that gets one beat in the time signature.

bending
Shifting the pitch of a note either higher or lower.

blow bend
An exhale bend that vibrates both reeds simultaneously to produce a bend effect that pulls the note down.

blue notes
Changes made to the major scale, specifically a flatted third and a flatted seventh note, that create harmonic tension between sounds usually identified with a major scale and a minor scale. A flatted fifth is also frequently used as an additional blue note.

blues scale

A variation of the pentatonic scale that adds a passing tone between the third and fourth notes, creating a six-note scale. In the key of C, the scale would be C E♭ F F♯ G B♭.

bump bend up

A blow bend that begins with the original note, bends it up, and then returns to the original note.

chart

This notation has the melody written out on the staff and chord symbols written above the staff, but no lyrics.

chord

Three or more notes played at the same time.

chord chart

Notation that has only the chord changes of the progression, written as chord symbols, with no melody shown.

chord melodies

Created by playing the notes above and below the main melody note to create the chords, forming a sound like a three-part harmony.

chord progression

A series of chords that are played to accompany the melody of a song.

chord symbol

A way of writing a chord in letter form, rather than as a stack of notes on the staff, such as "Gm7" for a G minor seventh chord.

chorus

One time through a chord progression, generally used to define the length, or number of choruses, of a solo.

chromatic

A scale with thirteen notes from octave to octave, which includes every possible note in the scale that exists between the two octaves.

circular breathing

A breathing technique that allows a musician to play a continuous stream of notes indefinitely.

clef symbol

The symbol tells you what notes the lines and spaces of the staff stand for.

comping

Short for complementing—playing in a way that supports and encourages a soloist.

consonance

A sound where all the notes are in tune with each other and form a stable, pleasant sound.

country scale

A variation of the major scale that's often used in country and folk music for its natural bouncy rhythm. It's played by selecting the first, second, third, fifth, sixth, and eighth (octave) notes of the major scale. The scale is also known as a major pentatonic scale.

cross harp

Selecting a harp tuned to the key three notes above the key of the song you want to play, and then playing in second position.

delay

Making a copy of your original sound and then repeating it after a short delay, hence the name.

diatonic

A scale with eight notes from octave to octave, which contains only the notes in the scale of the key being played.

dip bend down

A draw bend that begins with the original note, bends it down, and then returns to the original note.

direct box

A box that accepts your mic's ¼-inch plug and comes out with a three-pin balanced output jack, used to plug an instrument or microphone directly into a PA system.

dissonance

An unstable tonal quality where the combination of notes being played clash with each other and make the listener wish for resolution.

distortion

An effect created naturally by overdriving an amplifier to produce a long sustain, or created artificially by using an effects box.

dominant

The fifth degree of the scale.

Dorian mode

A minor scale that has a flatted third and a flatted seventh (but no flatted sixth as in the natural minor).

dotted note

When a dot appears after a note it means that the note is to be played for half again its usual time value. For example, a dot written after a half note, which normally gets two beats in 4/4 time, would now be played for three beats instead.

dotted rest

When a dot appears after a rest it means that the rest is to be held for half again its usual time value. For example, a dot written after a half rest, which normally gets held for two beats in 4/4 time, would now be held for three beats instead.

double bend down

A draw bend executed twice in rapid succession.

doubling

Using two voices to play the same note, phrase, or part.

draw bend

An inhale bend that pulls both the draw reed and the blow reed simultaneously, creating a new note that is neither of the reeds' natural tunings. The overall effect of a draw bend is always to pull the pitch of the note down.

draw harp

Selecting a harp tuned one note below the key of the song you want to play and then playing in third position.

dynamics

How loudly or softly you're playing.

ear training

A series of exercises that teach you the skill of listening to a note or phrase and then reproducing it on your instrument.

echo

The repeated reproduction of the original sound.

embouchure

The manner in which the inside of the mouth is adjusted relative to the mouthpiece of a wind instrument to create various effects.

ensemble playing

Playing music with other musicians in a duet or group setting.

fifth position

Begins on the 5 blow and enables you to play another type of minor scale known as the Phrygian mode.

first position

Playing the major scale that the harmonica is tuned to, usually focusing on holes 4, 5, 6, and 7 blow.

flat sign

Looks like this: ♭. When it's written directly in front of a note it means the note is to be lowered one half step below normal.

flatted note

A note that's lowered one half step.

fourth position

Begins on the 6 draw and enables you to play a natural minor scale in A when played on a C diatonic harmonica.

half step

The smallest space between two notes in Western music.

half-step down bend

A draw bend that bends the original note down one half step.

improvisation

The spontaneous creation of music in the immediate moment, played without any written music or notation for guidance.

interval

Two notes played at the same time.

key signature

This appears after the clef symbol in the first measure, and is expressed by one or more sharp signs or flat signs (one type or the other). Because every key has different notes that are always sharp or flat in its scale, these sharps or flats tell you that those notes will always be sharp or flat throughout the entire piece of music, unless otherwise indicated.

lead sheet

Also known as sheet music, this notation has the melody line written in notes on the staff, with chord symbols above the staff and the lyrics to the song written below the staff.

major pentatonic

A variation of the major scale that's often used in country and folk music for its natural bouncy rhythm. It's played by selecting the first, second, third, fifth, sixth, and eighth (octave) notes of the major scale. The scale is also known as a country scale.

melody

A succession of notes assembled to form a purposeful sequence.

metronome

A device, either mechanical or electronic, that establishes a steady, reliable beat.

modes

Classical scales that grew out of ancient Greek music. They are centered around the notes of a C major scale, and each of the seven modes uses the same consecutive notes of that C major scale—but each mode begins on a different note of that scale.

musical notation

Any written system of communicating how to play music.

natural sign

Looks like this: ♮. This sign is placed directly in front of a note when a note that's always supposed to be sharp or flat because of the key signature is instead to be played at its original pitch.

octave
Two notes with the same letter that are twelve half steps apart.

overblow
An exhale that jams one of the reeds while vibrating the other reed to create an overtone above the original note.

overdrive
Pushing a tube amp into saturation by turning the volume up to the maximum to produce a natural distortion.

overtone
A separate note created by the vibration caused by playing your original note.

phrase
A group of notes that expresses one musical idea.

phrasing
The way notes are articulated and assembled into groups. A phrase is a group of notes that expresses a musical thought or idea.

Phrygian mode
A minor scale that has a flatted second in addition to a flatted sixth and seventh.

playing by ear
The skill of being able to hear a melody, a song, or any piece of music and then being able to play it.

polyrhythm
Two or more rhythms being played at the same time.

position
The location on the harmonica where you begin to play, which is usually where the tonic (first note) of the scale is for the key of the song you're playing.

prebend
A bend that begins with the bent note and returns to the original note.

range
All of the notes that can be played on an instrument, from the lowest to the highest.

rest sign

Symbols that tell you how long you'll be resting (as opposed to playing) within each measure.

Whole rest:

Half rest:

Quarter rest:

Eighth rest:

Sixteenth rest:

regeneration

Having more than one echo repeat after your original sound because the output from the delay is being fed back into the input over and over again. This creates the sound of multiple echoes that fade in volume as they repeat.

reverb

Short for reverberation, which is the bouncing of sound waves off of many different surfaces in an enclosed space at one time.

riff

A series of notes that create a musical idea or phrase.

scale degree

The numerical position a note holds in a scale. Every chord has a root, a third, and a fifth.

second position

Playing the blues scale in the key a fifth above the key the harmonica is tuned to, focusing on holes 2, 3, 4, 5, and 6 draw.

sharp sign

Looks like this: ♯. When it's written directly in front of a note it means that note is to be raised one half step above normal.

shuffle

A rhythm in 4/4 time where each of the four beats in the measure is divided into triplets. The rhythm is then further refined by accenting just the first and last beat of each group of triplets. It sounds like "shuffle-shuffle-shuffle-shuffle."

slapback

The sound of an instrument bouncing once off the back wall of a room, giving your notes a concert-hall quality.

slur

Represented by a curved line over or under a group of notes, a group of notes played together smoothly with one note flowing directly into the next, as opposed to each note having a separate hard attack.

staccato

To hold a note or chord for as short a duration as possible, like a short burst of sound.

staff

The five vertical lines on which standard musical notation is written.

standard notation

The most common form of musical notation where all notes and chords are written on a staff of five vertical lines, and all the information you need to play the music—including what key the music is in, what the time signature is, what speed to play it, how loudly or softly to play it, and exactly how long to play each note—is precisely specified.

straight harp

Selecting a harp that's in the same key as the song you want to play and then playing the melody in first position.

subdominant

The fourth degree of the scale.

syncopation

The emphasizing of beats that are normally not the strong or accented beats in the rhythm you're playing.

tablature

A form of musical notation that tells you where on your instrument to put your fingers—or in the case of the harmonica, your lips. Because tablature is based on a representation of the physical instrument itself, it is specific to one instrument, so harmonica tablature is completely different from guitar tablature or bagpipe tablature. Besides telling which holes on the harp to use, harmonica tablature, or tab for short, tells you whether you should blow or draw that hole, and also whether you should bend the note or not.

tempo

The speed at which a piece of music is played.

third

An interval of two notes in a scale separated by one note.

third position

Playing the minor scale one note above the key the harmonica is tuned to, focusing on holes 4, 5, 6, and 7 draw.

tie

Represented by a curved line written between two notes of the same pitch, a tie means you are to hold the note for the total number of beats the two notes are worth together. For example, two half notes (each of which gets two beats) of the same pitch with a tie between them would be played as one note held for four beats.

time signature

The third thing that appears in the first measure after the clef symbol and the key signature. Expressed as two numbers, one above the other, the top number tells you how many beats are in each measure, and the bottom number tells you what kind of note gets counted as one beat. For example, in 3/4 time there are three beats per measure and the quarter note gets one beat. In 3/8 time there are three beats per measure and the eighth note gets one beat.

tongue shuffle

A technique that combines the techniques of tongue vamping, tongue slapping, octaves, and single notes to create a repeating shuffle rhythm.

tongue slapping

A technique that employs basic tongue blocking and adds the action of moving the tongue on and off of the comb to block and unblock holes in order to change the number of notes being played at one time.

tongue vamping

A technique that combines the techniques of tongue blocking and tongue slapping to create a repeating rhythmic pattern of alternating single notes and chord sounds.

tonic

The first note of a scale, and also the first note of the scale of the key the song is in.

treble clef

Signified by this symbol 𝄞, the lines of the staff from bottom to top represent E G B D F.

tremolo

A sound created by running the volume control of an amplifier through a slow wave form that uniformly raises and lowers the volume at an even pace. This subtle wavering of the volume overlays the sound with a pleasant texture.

triad

A three-note chord made up of the first, third, and fifth notes of a scale.

trill

Two notes played in rapidly alternating manner.

triplets

A rhythm where each individual beat in the measure is divided into three equal parts.

voicing

The order in which the notes of a chord are played.

whole-step down bend

A draw bend that bends the original note down one whole step.

INDEX

ABOUT THE AUTHORS

Blake Brocksmith is a harmonica player, singer, guitarist, actor, writer, and director. He has performed and recorded professionally on the harmonica since 1986.

Gary Dorfman is the chief engineer at Batcave Recording, working with nationally known artists including Rob Zombie, Kenny Garrett, and The Strokes. Mr. Dorfman lives in New York.

Douglas Lichterman is a musician, author, and music educator. In the 1970s he was a founding member of the rock band Windows, which opened for many of the top bands of the time, including Jefferson Starship and Jerry Garcia. Mr. Lichterman is the coauthor of *The About.com Guide to Acoustic Guitar*. He lives in St. Petersburg, Florida.